"Anxiety is constrictive and will lead people of faith away from celebrating the precious gift of life and living together. The Rev. Dr. Jim Bailiff gives voice to opportunity and the possibilities that are ours when we are able to trust in God's care for us."

—The Rev. Karen Wismer, Co-pastor of Pine Shores Presbyterian Church in Sarasota, Florida

"Anxiety is a real part of our lives. Though often seen as a condition to be healed by medication, Jim Bailiff instead offers a healing based on meditation. A radical trust in the power and presence of God allows us to live in grace with ourselves, and compassion with others and nature. Faith does transform anxiety."

—The Rev. Dr. Chuck Moffett, Chaplain of Bay Village in Sarasota, Florida

"*Anxiety Yields to Faith* is a masterful, coherent, and well-thought-out analysis of the persistent though sometimes elusive presence of anxiety. Almost every epoch of our human history could be labeled 'The Age of Anxiety.' Through his far-reaching knowledge of the most varied perspectives of historical personalities and movements, as well as ample support in the Holy Scriptures and anecdotal accounts, Bailiff enlightens our quest for peace of heart and peace of mind. With the assurance of divine compassion, the reader gains insight into the progressive discovery of the therapeutic value of faith and the liberating power of God."

—Paul Ciholas, PhD, retired professor of History
of Ideas from the University of Kentucky and
retired director of the Institute for Liberal
Studies at Kentucky State University

Anxiety
YIELDS TO
Faith

Anxiety YIELDS TO Faith

Reflections on How **FAITH** *Helps Us Control Our Anxiety*

JAMES D. BAILIFF

Published in the United States of America

ISBN 978-1-962730-47-1 (SC)

JDB Publishing
222 West 6th Street
Suite 400, San Pedro, CA, 90731
retrev1@frontier.com

Order Information and Rights Permission:

Quantity sales. Special discounts might be available on quantity purchases by corporations, associations, and others. For details, contact the publisher at the address above.

For Book Rights Adaptation and other Rights Permission.
Call us at toll-free 1-888-945-8513 or send us an email at admin@stellarliterary.com.

ABOUT THE AUTHOR

A native of North Carolina, Dr. Bailiff is a retired pastor. He and his wife, Beverly, have six out-of the-nest children, seventeen grandchildren, and two great grandchildren, along with Moose, a ten year old, five and a half pound Yorkshire Terrier.

Bailiff holds bachelor degrees from Johnson University and East Tennessee State University, a Master of Theology from Vanderbilt University and a Doctor of Ministry from Emory University.

In retirement he has a special interest in writing. His first book, *Mining for Meaning,* published in 2013, focuses upon harvesting rich veins of meaning from our relationship with God, one another and nature. In this second work, *Anxiety Yields to Faith*, he explores the dynamics of faith and challenges readers to utilize them in dealing with their anxiety.

Jim and Beverly live in Sarasota, Florida where they are engaged in the music ministry of the congregation in which they are active. Both enjoy numerous visits with their children and their families, summer vacations in the mountains, and occasional international travel. He is an avid golfer at their local club and takes delight in golf's opportunities to fellowship with old friends and meet new ones.

CONTENTS

FOREWORD

. . . .

It has been both my privilege and opportunity to have shared a personal and professional relationship with the author of this book, Dr. James D. Bailiff. We have been joined together in the faith since first meeting at Vanderbilt University Divinity School in 1964.

Dr. Bailiff is affectionately known as Jim to family and parishioners, friends and neighbors. He has spent over 50 years in Christian Ministry, both with congregations of The Christian Church (Disciples of Christ) and the larger field of service on state and national levels. He is a consummate thinker with a matching theological tenacity and a clear vision of pastoral ministry and care.

This volume will reveal to its readers Jim's personal belief—born and nurtured by loving parents and by participation with servant churches—that we are all held in the crucible of God's never-ending steadfastness and love.

The hypothesis upon which this document is founded insists that insecurities, both externally and internally are the troubling "breeding ground for anxiety" which, without an intervening faith, leaves humankind drifting on a sea of irresolution.

The issue Jim explores with readers is how to engage life—above and beyond the transient normal and everyday experiences of anxiety—to find resolution to that deeper anxiety which threatens and has the potential to render us extremely vulnerable and hopeless. Supported by relevant Scripture and parable-like personal stories, the author artfully weaves together a tapestry that reveals to the reader how to have wheels placed under one's faith. Each chapter has within it the profound possibility to catch the reader up in something unique and faith-infusing.

I invite you to become acquainted with Jim's conviction as he reaches the conclusion that one's personal faith is perhaps the most potent weapon we are granted with which to defeat anxiety.

I know of no studies that render percentages about the number of human beings who suffer with anxiety. But, as a

Fellow in the *American Association of Pastoral Counselors* and Clinician in the *American Association of Marriage and Family Therapists*, I have found that anxiety is extremely present within the core of most of those seeking clarification and resolution.

Jim believes that the power of God's grace and our response to this mysterious gift lead to profound transformation. I believe you will experience the power of transformation on your own as you engage this work.

Full of hope, the author has his finger on the pulse of human possibilities when fully engaged in spiritual awareness. Enjoy this solid work of theological and spiritual discernment.

David G. Brown Jr., D. Min.

March 31, 2015

ACKNOWLEDGEMENTS

I have deep appreciation for academia. Early on my teachers helped me to learn the basics. Subsequently they motivated me to behold and explore the wide expanses of life and learning. It was then that I began to sense the great movements of history and the diversity of cultures, the keen insights of various schools of psychology, and the profound issues of philosophy and theology.

One of my most stimulating motivators for learning was Mrs. George Shook, a high school teacher, who challenged me to focus my thinking and to expand my vision. Visiting her in her home in Johnson City, Tennessee in the summer of 2000, I was able to express my appreciation directly to her. Significantly, I left that visit with my arms full of books, beloved gifts from her library.

But the larger laboratory for my learning has been outside the walls of academia, among people in every day life—people in civic organizations, community service boards, religious congregations, family systems, and sports events. There I have encountered the issues with which most folk struggle and have experienced growing levels of trust leading to dialogue and healing insights. In any helping profession, if one is adequately trained, she or he enters a lifetime of learning through interaction with folk encountered in everyday life. This has been my experience. I express heartfelt thanks for so many of these persons with whom I have engaged across the decades.

My wife, Beverly, not only encourages my writing, but graciously gives me the space for it. Our grown children are always asking. "Dad, what are you writing about now?" These, along with colleagues in the practice of ministry off whom I bounce questions in a search for accuracy, relevance, and clarity, continue to bless my thought and actions. Among these are the late Reverend Alan Bond and my co-pastors The Reverend Dr. Bruce Wismer and The Reverend Karen Wismer.

Specifically related to this publication I am indebted to Beverly and her availability for conversation regarding my writing focus, for a sister parishioner, Allison Vance and her meticulous focus upon proof reading, and for my long-time colleague, the Reverend Dr. David Brown, whose vast practice in the field of pastoral psychotherapy has equipped him to offer important critique of my focus upon anxiety and faith.

Finally, I feel deep gratitude for God's Spirit whose presence continuously keeps me sensitive to the needs of people and the relevance of faith in dealing with those needs.

INTRODUCTION

. . . .

Insecurity, always in attack mode, is all around and within us. It is the breeding ground for anxiety so intense that it cannot be dormant. As an erupting volcano spews its lava, insecurity belches its anxiety everywhere.

We are told that anxiety is the most common mental malady in the United States as approximately forty million adults are affected by it. Some experience it in relation to specific issues and struggles. Others experience more complicated anxiety *disorders* which represent an overreaction to a situation that is usually only subjective and not real—fear of being in public places, fear of heights, closed places, etc.

Although there are those within most every community for whom the issue of where the next meal is coming from is paramount, for most of us insecurity is rooted in other issues such as lack of meaning and purpose, the complexity of steering children through the minefield of substance abuse, vulnerability to serious disease, the specter of financial failure, the agitation of international friction, terrorism, and damaged relationships.

In chapter One I, titled "The Balance and Imbalance in Human Beings," I consider how we human beings are a *mixture* of emotional and spiritual balance and imbalance. Some level of anxiety resides in most everyone and possesses enough power to throw us off balance.

Of course, there are times in which anxiety serves in positive ways, preventing us from touching a hot stove or from carelessly exposing ourselves to a high crime area. But we also know deeper levels of anxiety with destructive capacity to bind and block us from fulfilling our potential. This book takes the destructive edge of those anxiety levels seriously and explores them both as *psychological* and *spiritual* phenomena.

There are multiple options for the treatment of anxiety as a *psychological* issue ranging from various contexts of "talking therapy" to "pharmacological therapy." While affirming those, my focus here is to explore the *spiritual* dimensions of anxiety and the healing power of faith through a process of "spiritual therapy."

If done well, spiritual therapy utilizes so many of the helpful insights and techniques of other types of therapies and sees itself in alliance with them toward the goal of human wholeness. It specializes in understanding the dynamics of authentic faith and how those dynamics can become resources for persons who are struggling with anxiety. My practice of pastoral counseling and care convinces me that the person whose world view is informed and shaped by faith can expect remarkable results in her or his desire to reduce and eventually neutralize anxiety's destructive power.

As a result, this work at times is heavy on the spiritual side of the treatment equation. But my aim is to do spiritual therapy that reflects awareness of viewing a person in terms of wholeness. By wholeness I mean the human being as a combination of body, mind, and spirit woven together into an integral, inseparable entity. This approach is distinct from those based on the dualistic notion that the body and the soul are two different entities separated from one another into watertight compartments in such a way that it is assumed that one can be accessed to the exclusion of the other.

Viewing a human being as whole (holistically) paves the way for affirming the validity of various disciplines in treating anxiety as long as each of those disciplines is aware that a human being possesses physical, mental, and spiritual dimensions bound together interdependently. Thus in the pastoral counseling role of my ministry, I have found it useful to be aware of my client's physical, mental and spiritual state and, when possible, to be in dialogue with her or his other health specialists in appropriate ways.

Firmly committed to the effectiveness of faith in the treatment of anxiety, I attempt to lead readers into a serious engagement with faith, not as commitment to a particular *belief system*, but an experience of *radical trust* in God capable of producing in us a *transforming experience* that leads to positive action (service) in which we affirm and bless God's created order. Moreover, I perceive both the fellowship with God and the action through which it gets expressed to be therapeutic. Readers will discover a more detailed treatment of this experience in chapters two and three titled "Faith Connects Us to God (Therapeutic Faith)" and "Faith Connects Us to the World" (Therapeutic Work)." When we experience the connection of our faith and work we enter a zone of living that blesses us with amazing power to free us from bondage to insecurity and its anxiety.

Finally, let me share my deep appreciation for you who read this work. It is my sincere hope that it will result in improved balance in your life.

Jim Bailiff

CHAPTER ONE

How Balanced Are We Human Beings?

"We are, after all, lumps of clay, There are brittle pieces, hard pieces. We have little shape or beauty. But we need not despair. If we are clay, let us remember there is a Potter, and His wheel."

Peter Marshall

Balance and Imbalance

Most likely we have all experienced both very cold and hot temperatures. For me, the coldest were encountered during those years of growing up in the mountains of North Carolina. The winter temperatures were often well below freezing resulting in a thick layer of ice growing over Curtis Creek that flowed by our house.

My primary morning chore was milking our family cow. We called her Patsy, a gentle Guernsey whose body bore the beautiful markings of light tan spattered across an underlying sea of white. On winter mornings I followed a ritual of putting on a heavy flannel shirt, a pair of thick trousers, heavy socks and high top shoes; followed by slipping into my heavy coat and rubber boots.

Off I would go, shuffling for about 200 yards through the snow to Patsy's night-time home in the barn. Entering her stall, I would halter and lead her into the breezeway, her steaming breath rising like the exhaust from the pipes of an eighteen wheeler. There I would position my milking stool, remove my gloves, place my hands on her teats, and proceed to massage her milk into my bucket as she stood in position for a ritual she had long since internalized. During the milking process both Patsy and I were exposed to the extreme chill of the winter wind that rushed through the breezeway. It was then that I experienced the coldest temperatures I can remember.

The return trip through the snow back to our house was often testy but my anticipation of home and hearth sped me toward its warmth. Arriving, I shed the heavy coat and boots, moved toward the radiating heat of our generous coal-fed stove, and began the process of "thawing out." Even though I felt frozen my body temperature was remarkably stable with a temperature around 98.5 degrees.

Then there is the issue of heat. When I think of heat, my memory rushes back a few years to a time when my wife and I, along with several friends, were visiting the pyramids at Giza in Egypt. Walking across the burning sand from one to the other we experienced a temperature hovering around 110 degrees. As I sipped my bottled water and struggled to put one foot in front of the other, I remember yearning for the summertime high country of the Rocky or Appalachian mountains.

At the main pyramids, I remember entering and descending into the relative coolness of ancient chambers insulated by thick layers of stone and tons of desert sand. There we comfortably enjoyed the ancient artistic imagery and the excellent commentary of our tour guide.

As we emerged from those chambers, the searing desert heat again smacked our faces and locked our bodies in uncomfortable embrace. But we trudged on tolerating its unpleasantness in order to experience not only Giza but the legendary Valley of the Kings which, together with the pyramids, constitutes one of the most fascinating cradles of history in the world.

But Egypt's hot sun did not suppress the ability of our bodies to keep our temperatures around 98.5 degrees. The inspiration of such physical stability was, for me, almost as inspiring as the day's scenes upon which we reflected in the comfort of our air conditioned hotel room.

The temperature constancy of our bodies in cold or heat is recognized as an important reflection of *homeostasis*, that state of physiological equilibrium produced by a balance of functions and chemical composition within an organism. The homeostatic balance of our bodies has inspired me since, as a child, I learned about it in my elementary education health classes.

But that balance is vulnerable. We know about those times whose extraordinary conditions produce extreme temperatures capable of penetrating our homeostatic balance and plunging us into abnormally low body temperature (hypothermia) or abnormally high body temperature (hyperthermia). Thankfully, these extremes are exceptions to the norm in which our bodies have the ability to maintain their balance under ordinary temperature extremities.

Let's adjust our focus slightly to ask about our emotional and spiritual constitution. Do we have homeostatic balance there similar to that in our physical dimension? If so, is that balance vulnerable to extreme conditions just as our bodies are?

Indeed, our emotional and spiritual dimensions seem to have a fairly robust homeostatic balance. Most of us cope pretty well with everyday stresses. We perform our daily duties and move through our routines quite well. Despite life's normal stresses we are able to remain functional. To that extent the homeostatic principle seems to be at work in the emotional and spiritual dimensions of our being.

However, our balance there seems to be more vulnerable to the unbalancing threat of extraordinary pressures. When such pressures come upon us with their enormous force we can quickly lose that balance. For example, when challenges come from such potentially stressful experiences as hunger, natural disasters, hostility from other people, loss of jobs, financial downturns, injustice, the death of loved ones, or devastating disease, our emotional/spiritual balance often staggers under their severe weight.

In this talk about balance and imbalance in all dimensions of our being, I am simply reminding all of us that we possess a natural balance that enables us to function with a modicum of satisfaction under normal circumstances. But the reality of life is that we are constantly confronted with extraordinary circumstances capable of destroying us. Therefore we are perpetually in danger of being overwhelmed and rendered dysfunctional.

What is our response as we hear such talk of our vulnerability? Few of us can simply slough it off with a "such is life" response. When we really think about personal vulnerability our insecurity comes to awareness along with that which always spews from it—considerable anxiety. At some point(s) in our lives most of us struggle with this anxiety. It is upon that experience of anxiety and its management that I wish to focus.

Throughout my pastoral career I have observed that while some people seem to possess remarkable coping power in face of life's pressures, others seem to fall apart. Wherever one may be on this coping spectrum I think it is safe to say that most of us attempt to deal with our anxiety. But, as sand in a mechanical gear system, the sheer weight of our anxiety-producing insecurity negatively affects the efficiency of our coping mechanisms.

While some anxiety may be useful, the large injections one receives at the hand of crises like those mentioned above complicate the situation by clouding our vision and contaminating our decision-making process.

Let me repeat: wherever we are on the coping spectrum—some coping better than others—we all experience a great deal of anxiety, especially when we face critical challenges, and attempt to deal with them.

I wish to illustrate with stories of two persons, one crushed by anxiety and the other able to cope.

Laura's (not her real name) Story

At church one Sunday morning a young couple told me of a friend who had fallen into deep depression. When they asked me to visit her that afternoon, I agreed to do so if they got her permission. That done, I went to her home and found her in deep distress, but willing and able to talk.

Laura told me of her relationship with a lover in which she had felt extremely insecure for months. Recently, he had announced that he no longer wanted to be with her. While not surprised at his dissatisfaction, she was stunned when he ended the relationship abruptly. She indicated that she could not imagine life without him and questioned whether she could exist apart from him.

It was obvious that she had fallen into deep despair and was contemplating suicide. Her description: "I have lost all hope. While I appreciate your coming to see me, I know of nothing you can say or do that will make it better."

She talked extensively but each word seemed to drag her further into the depths of her despair.

I spoke to her about the love her two friends had for her, the ones who had arranged our meeting. Moreover, I talked some about the love of God that always surrounds us, even when our senses do not pick up on it. Occasionally she seemed to grab onto such love talk, but soon would detach and sink again.

"I have lost all hope," became a repeated mantra throughout out conversation.

At one point I encouraged her to let me take her to the hospital.

Vehemently she resisted and warned me not to attempt forcing her to go. She was growing very tired and seemed no longer to desire my presence. I asked if she would like a prayer to which she consented. Taking her hand, I prayed for her.

"That was nice. Thank you for coming," she said. As I left, I felt a cloud of uneasiness around me.

Later that evening I heard from my friends that Laura had taken her life. Both they and I were extremely sad that our intervention had not changed the course of her journey into self-destruction.

On Wednesday I received a letter from Laura in which she expressed what sounded like sincere gratitude: "Thank you so much for coming and spending time with me. Your listening ears were refreshing. Your prayer had the sound of genuine compassion. Your faith in God's love was clear. I just wish I could share such faith, hope, and love but I cannot. By the time you receive this letter I will have taken my life. I'm sorry. Please forgive me."

As I reflect upon that very painful experience with Laura, it seems that her journey into despair, her insecurity, her angst had not only numbed her to any inner strength she had but had also blinded her to the One who could have fanned any embers of hope in order to couple divine power with her human strength for deliverance.

I imagine her life ended with a sense of sinking into oblivion. She felt lost and wanted to end it. It helps me to know that, though she did not sense God, God was there embracing her in loving care. My hope is that she now rests in the peace of God.

John's (not his real name) Story

John was a wonderful friend whose life seemed to be as balanced as any I have witnessed. The credibility of his character and his winsome ways enabled him to have considerable influence upon others, influence he used for good. His faith in God was strong and expressed itself in his compassion for those who were "down and out." Very successful financially, he was able to live comfortably, to give extravagant financial support to his church, and to aid causes he felt were noble. Wisdom oozed from his every pore and he possessed an uncanny stability.

Then came a point at which he was diagnosed with a rare and serious form of cancer. His physicians at the M.D. Anderson Clinic in Texas indicated that they had seen only four other cases of this particular strain and that their treatment had not been successful.

Their prognosis was not positive.

During that period I observed my friend closely. The information he had received from his physicians had a notable impact upon him. I saw him stagger under its weight. He shared with me that his anxiety was at the highest level he had ever experienced. Clearly he was struggling with this new sense of gaping vulnerability. His usual calm had become a churning sea; yet he trusted God.

Over the approximate year and a half of his struggle, I witnessed his physical decline but, simultaneously, I could see him fine-tuning his spiritual sensitivity and coping more effectively with his physical demise.

Though anxiety was present, its effect upon him seemed less potent than in Laura's case. It didn't have a knock out punch. His attitude was very much like that of St. Paul who wrote:

> *"But this precious treasure—this light and power within us—is held in a perishable container, that is, in our weak bodies. Everyone can see that the glorious power within must be from God and is not our own. We are pressed on every side by troubles, but not crushed and broken. We are perplexed because we don't know why things happen as they do, but we don't give up and quit. We are hunted down, but God never abandons us. We get knocked down, but we get up again and keep going. These bodies of ours are constantly facing death, just as Jesus did, so it is clear that it is only the living Christ within [who keeps us safe]"* (2 Corinthians 4:7-10 —The Living Bible).

John seemed aware that while his physical dimension was in sure decline there was something within him that was growing more robust. He spoke of it this way, "While there is no question that my elevator is going down, I meet myself on another elevator going up!"

That observation reminded me of another inspiring symbol of life's destiny penned by St. Paul:

"Even though our physical being is gradually decaying, yet our spiritual being is renewed day after day. And this small and temporary trouble we suffer will bring us a tremendous and eternal glory, much greater than the trouble. For we fix our attention, not on things that are seen, but on things that are unseen. What can be seen lasts only for a time, but what cannot be seen lasts forever"
(2 Corinthians 4:16b-18—Today's English Version).

Can you see the different dynamics at play in Laura's and John's stories? They responded to their anxiety in vastly different ways.

Laura allowed her anxiety to dominate her and become a ghastly experience that ushered her into self-destruction. Not only did it destroy her inner strength to cope but it succeeded in blinding her to the life-line God was tossing to her in the midst of her tumult.

John, on the other hand, while feeling the strength of anxiety and its power to stagger him, never experienced total dissipation of inner strength nor blindness to Providential care.

Daily he exposed himself to the love and care of God, the *higher* power, which magnified his *inner* strength and amplified God's *divine* strength. Drawing upon both sources, he was able to live and to die with a deep sense of meaning.

As you consider the different dynamics of these stories please do not conclude that Laura's life was less valuable than John's. Even though Laura became a victim of her anxiety and John a victor over his, they were and are loved equally by God who has received them on the other side.

In both Laura's and John's experiences one is able to grasp the presence of significant anxiety and its effects upon the human psyche. Some of us have known the circumstances these two faced. Others of us, while not facing their precise situation, have experienced other crises that have triggered anxiety storms. We all seem to know that strong anxiety, if not raging directly in our lives, lies just below the surface and possesses significant power to affect our lives negatively.

Seeking a Better Understanding of Anxiety

Let us turn to this anxiety phenomenon and try better to understand it. We have witnessed anxiety's power to throw us off balance. We know, too, that anxiety is not some strange phenomenon that affects only others in far away places. From a time perspective, we seem to know that anxiety is not some new thing that has come to affect only modern folk.

The anxiety dynamic has been with us at every stage of our development as a species. Anthropological and archaeological studies suggest that anxiety is as old as the earliest human beings who had to grapple with one another and nature in an attempt to secure their existence. On the walls of ancient caves we see the drama of such struggle among our ancestors.

We certainly find references to anxiety in both the Old and New Testaments of the Bible. There is a particular word for it in Hebrew, *deagaa* which is reflected in David's prayer, "*Search me, O God, and know my heart; test me and know my anxious thought*" (Psalm 139:23). The word for "anxious" or "anxiety" in Greek is *merimna* reflected, for example, in St. Paul's admonition, "*Do not be anxious about anything, but in everything, by prayer and petition, with thanksgiving, present your requests to God*" (Philippians 4:6—Revised Standard Version).

When Darwin (1809-1882) spoke of the "origin of species" and the "survival of the fittest" listeners could imagine the strains and stresses down through history that gave rise to vigorous anxiety; particularly within species that, like humans, reflected consciousness.

Anxiety is very much a part of human history. But I'm convinced that the 20th century, whose findings continue to be recognized and explored in our time, made an even clearer case for its prevalence and power.

To my mind, two movements from that period contributed to this clearer vision: One was the combination of the *psychoanalytic* movement, spawned by Sigmund Freud (1865-1939), along with the depth psychology movement that followed in his wake. Another was the *existentialist* movement rooted in the 19th century work of Danish theologian Soren Kierkegaard (1813-1855) and German philosopher Friedrich Nietzsche (1844-1900) and popularized in the works of Jean Paul Sartre (1905-1980) and Albert Camus (1913-1960).

Aware of the multi-layered character of human consciousness Freud developed his tools of psychoanalysis as a way of exploring those layers and their depths. In the process he became more aware of and sensitive to the forceful drives and the behavior-affecting anxieties that lie deep within us.

While some of Freud's methods and conclusions remain debated, there is widespread agreement that he properly fixed our attention on the depth and complexity of the human psyche. His insights have convinced us that our misbehavior is rooted in something considerably deeper than mere choice and that its treatment requires considerably more than mere admonitions to get ourselves straightened out.

Existentialism, more philosophical and theological in nature than psychoanalysis, emerged and grew in influence. Embracing diverse doctrines, it focused upon an analysis of individual existence in what it saw as an unfathomable universe. Generally it emphasized the uniqueness and isolation of the individual experience in a universe that was either indifferent or hostile. Existentialism stressed freedom of choice and responsibility for the consequences of one's acts and emphasized that with this freedom and responsibility come profound *angst* and *dread.*

Still very much alive in our own time, these "depth" movements in psychology and existentialism have deeply influenced the fields of psychology, philosophy and theology. But their influence has expanded beyond those traditional arenas to become more widely reflected in literature and the arts.

We are now clearer that human life, though a beautiful gift, is fraught with problems which validate the ancient view that humanity is caught up in a complex predicament. Examining that predicament either from a psychological, philosophical or theological angle of vision we are now more aware that our dilemma is considerably more profound and complex than our civilization had earlier imagined. We are more convinced than ever of the pervasiveness of anxiety within each person and its power to block our way from becoming whole. As a result our search for mental health, for meaning, and for redemption is much more informed than before.

While most of us are functional in our living, the ice on which we skate, which separates functionality from dysfunctionality, seems thin under the lead-like weight of our extensive anxiety.

The voices around (and often *within* us) offer convincing clues:

"I don't know how much longer I can hang on."

"I feel like my world is about to cave."

"I'm really worried about myself, my family and my world." "I can't find rest or peace and sleeping is difficult."

Survivalists at heart, most of us want to cope, and we try. But so often our efforts are weak and temporary. Consider, for example, the story of a couple preparing to host good friends. They were anticipating an evening with dinner and conversation followed by a card game. Preparation included making their home presentable and placing the dog in a comfortable place in the basement. The final touch was to turn on the sound of soft music to form the perfect background.

When the doorbell rang the friends greeted one another with fond embrace. Hearing the exchange the dog became excited and began barking at a volume well above the sound of the soft music. The host's solution was simply to turn up the music's volume to a level that drowned out the barking.

All went well. The evening was a life-giving experience. But when the guests had departed and the background music was turned off there is was, the sound of the barking dog.

With some imagination we can catch an important insight. We try to drown out the sounds of our anxiety (the panic of its insecurity and the confusion of its aimlessness) with materialism, consumerism, preoccupation with hi tech gadgets, and abuse of mind-altering substances. But in those telling moments when their "noise" has stopped, there it is—the persistent "barking" of unmet needs down deep within us churned by the anxiety emerging from our insecurity.

Our noisy preoccupations succeed only temporarily in drowning out our barking dog. Eventually we must confront and deal with the continuing angst deep within if we are to become whole.

The spectrum of anxiety is wide, ranging from "normal" to those forms with power to do us harm; including those various anxiety disorders.

Normal anxiety recognizes real dangers and triggers appropriate fear and flight reactions. For example in face of a tornado, we seek secure shelter.

Such precaution is normal and necessary.

But anxiety becomes a negative force when it causes us to become suspicious of and competitive with others, seeking to outdo them in order to secure our own position. For example, we may dangerously speed through traffic in order to get ahead of another driver or rapidly accelerate our pace of shopping in order to be first at the check out counter. By such action we show our anxiety about our position relative to others, along with our deep worry that we may be on the losing end when the dust has settled.

Beyond these points on the anxiety spectrum there are troubling anxiety disorders into which we may fall, experiencing a persistent gnawing in our gut for no identifiable reason. For example, I have a good friend who, at one point in his life, got extremely anxious when he went to a shopping mall to acquire some essentials. In therapy he voiced his feeling that everyone there was looking at and evaluating him. He related how it seemed that he was suddenly the center of critical attention for everyone around him. As a consequence he stopped going to public places and chose to become reclusive. One of the most important insights he received in his therapy was the unreality of his sense that he was the center of the universe's critical attention.

Though prevalent and powerful, anxiety can be managed. Treatments for it range from various forms of medication to different "talking" therapies such as one- to-one conservation with a trained counselor or participation in group therapy. There are times when a combination of these has proven to be helpful.

I am convinced that anxiety is experienced and expressed in multiple ways, that it comes with varying degrees of intensity, and that there is help to be gleaned from a multi-disciplined approach to treatment.

The Therapeutic Value of Faith in Dealing with Anxiety

With that understanding, let me remind you that this book has a particular focus, namely, the therapeutic value of *faith* (in a Judeo-Christian context) in dealing with our anxiety.[1] My aim, therefore, is to explore some avenues offered by faith which enable us to manage our anxiety more effectively. My hope is that the process will help us to see how faith provides us more internal security (peace within) while, at the same time, showing us styles of living in response to our exterior world which complement this inner peace.

To this point I have attempted to show that we are provided a physical and spiritual constitution which enables us to maintain constancy under *ordinary* circumstances. We have conceded that, while strong, our constitution is vulnerable to *extreme* situations.

I repeat my view that our natural emotional/ spiritual dimensions seem more vulnerable than our physical to being thrown off balance. Persons who can easily sustain their body's temperatures in cold and heat, may find they are less able to sustain such balance emotionally and spiritually when confronted with life's challenges, many of which are capable not only of throwing us off balance but of spiraling us into an abyss of despair.

Now I want to consider with you how faith can reduce the negative power of anxiety's potentially deadly grip; thereby setting us free to experience a better qualify of life.

That's the focus of the next two chapters in which I describe the therapeutic value of faith which expresses itself through an intentional reliance upon God (Chapter Two) and through answering the invitation of God to join in the therapeutic work of improving the world (Chapter Three). Together, the faith (trust) and work of God constitute two sides of the same coin designed to liberate us for abundant living.

CHAPTER TWO

· ·

Faith Connects Us to God
(Therapeutic Faith)

"A simple, childlike faith in a Divine Friend solves
all the problems that come to us by land or sea."
Helen Keller

In this chapter I invite you to explore with me the dynamics of becoming connected with God and how that connection enables us to deal successfully with anxiety and its negative effects.

Insights from Jesus

A helpful way to begin this exploration is to consider some insights on the issue provided in Jesus' *Sermon on the Mount* found in the Gospel of Matthew chapters 5-7.

A quick review of the sermon's contents will introduce us to the various themes Jesus addresses from which we can proceed, for our purpose, to choose the aspects upon which to focus: He begins the sermon with a recital of beatitudes (blessings) that produce happiness.

Following the beatitudes are two parables, one of salt and the other of light. From there he spotlights several issues which are considered important for the crowd gathered to receive his teaching. There is a total of twenty one issues.

All are important. But since it is our purpose to explore how faith helps us to overcome anxiety, the one that leaps out at us is his statement regarding that struggle. Let's zoom in on that one.

Before elaborating, he opens the subject with an astounding exhortation: *"…I tell you, do not be anxious about your life…"* (6:25a—Revised Standard Version). Another rendering offers: *"…do not be worried…*(Today's English Version).

Jesus' counsel sounds simple enough—some may say it's *simplistic.* Consider, for example, the times we have heard a person say to a really troubled friend or acquaintance, "Oh, don't worry. Everything's gonna be all right." Is that what Jesus is doing here? Serious reflection will show us that Jesus is not coming from such shallow triteness.

As we have seen, anxiety is one of humanity's foundational problems, one that has been a part of our emotional and spiritual constitution throughout the history of our development. It haunted our ancestors—both ancient and recent—and continues to haunt us. Anxiety is rooted in a deep sense of insecurity fed by the perception that everyone and everything around us is seeking an advantage over us. Thus, it arms us with an adversarial and competitive spirit that seeks to confront those threats with attempts to outperform them in acquiring the things needed to establish our own security.

Anxiety has the power to produce not only an intense suspicion of other *people*, but of the rest of *nature* as well; particularly nature's ravages against which we must protect ourselves at all cost.

Sometimes anxiety perceives *God* as out to get us as well, and attempts to convince us that we must outwit God in order to establish our own security.

It is not difficult for us to see that anxiety has the power to dwarf our potential for greatness by producing in us a paranoia that blocks us from the very sources that can nurture us toward wholeness, namely our fellow human beings, the natural world, and God.

Many of us have family members who are afflicted with anxiety. Not a few of us find infected pockets of it in our own lives. Billions of hours and dollars are invested in various kinds of therapies to help us deal with it.

In face of this monster what counsel does Jesus offer? "*Don't be anxious…!*" "*Don't be worried…!*" Is he serious?! Is he being audaciously cavalier toward one of our most destructive enemies?! Even though Jesus was and is held in high esteem, some question why he reflects such apparent casualness toward anxiety.

Before we simply react to these questions, let's allow them to settle in upon us. Let's genuinely listen to them and consider what lies behind them. It may just be that they can press us to explore where Jesus is coming from, the reasons lying behind his counsel not to worry and be anxious.

I sincerely believe that going deeper into Jesus' thinking on the subject of anxiety may reveal his comment to be much more profound than a surface evaluation may show.

Let's frame our exploration of his comments with this question: What is the "world view" that forms the basis for his counsel not to worry and be anxious? All we know about Jesus from the Holy Scriptures, Sacred Tradition, and the experience of many other authentic voices who have spoken of him, suggests that the foundational point of his world view was this: God is the *central reality* of the universe. God, the central reality, is also the *Creator who is superior to all creation.* There's more: God, the central reality and Creator *possesses pure love for all* creation. God *knows its needs and has the power* to meet them. Moreover, *God has designed a process in which all creation is constantly being transformed* into the wholeness and perfection that God intends.

Reflect upon the influences that led Jesus to this world view. Remember that he was reared in a family of faith and became a highly sensitized person of faith. From childhood he examined the traditions of Israel and became extremely knowledgeable of it's scriptures. Early on he opened and disciplined himself in developing a personal relationship with God. As a twelve year old boy he had engaged some of Israel's religious leaders in discussion of Hebrew tradition and faith. It is recorded that they recognized his remarkable insights and spiritual charisma.

Throughout, Jesus affirmed the faith that God is not detached or aloof from the created world but very close. Out of his acquaintance with Hebrew scripture, he identified with those passages—like the following great Psalm —that speak of God's mastery over and intimacy with creation:

> *"Lord, you have examined me and you know me. You know everything I do, from far away you understand all of my thoughts. You see me, whether I am working or resting, you know all my actions. Even before I speak, you already know what I will say. You are all around*

me on every side; your protect me with your power. Your knowledge of me is too deep; it is beyond my understanding.

Where could I go to escape from you? Where could I get away from your presence? If I went up to heaven, you would be there; if I lay down in the world of the dead, you would be there. If I flew away beyond the east or lived in the farthest place in the west, you would be there to help me. I could ask the darkness to hide me or the light around me to turn into night, but even darkness is not dark for you, and the night is as bright as the day. Darkness and light are the same to you.

You created every part of me; you put me together in my mother's womb….When I was growing there in secret, you knew that I was there—you saw me before I was born…" (Psalm 139:1-13, 15b-16—Today's English Version).

For Jesus this profound insight into God's primacy over and proximity to creation—including us human beings—is one of the fundamental realities of life.

Consider another of his foundational affirmations regarding God: God is not only at the center of life, God is there for the purpose of nurturing us to become everything we are designed to be. No doubt Jesus' respect for the insights of another great psalm strengthened his conviction about the caring nature of God:

"The Lord is my shepherd, I shall not want; he makes me lie down in green pastures. He leads me beside still waters; he restores my soul. He leads me in paths of righteousness for his name's sake.

Even though I walk through the valley of the shadow of death, I fear no evil; for thou art with me; thy rod and thy staff, they comfort me.

You prepare a table before me in the presence of my enemies; you anoint my head with oil, my cup overflows.

Surely goodness and mercy shall follow me all the days of my life; and I shall dwell in the house of the Lord my whole life long" (Psalm 23—Revised Standard Version).

I suspect Jesus had memorized this psalm and on more than one occasion repeated it as a source of God's promise to provide for our every need, including walking with us *through* the valley of the shadow of death all the way to the point at which we walk *out of it* .

The psalm assumes God's position as Creator and God's superiority over creation enabling God to participate in its process in such a way that the created universe, in spite of its imperfections, is on its way to being made whole and perfect, reflecting the Creator's intention for it. Perhaps this psalm's beautiful and caring imagery inspired Jesus to adopt its central symbol—Caring Shepherd—as the metaphor for describing his relationship with his followers: *"I am the good shepherd who is willing to die for the sheep"* (John 10:11—Today's English Version).

Jesus shared the heritage of a great faith tradition that emphasized both God's nearness and care. Understanding and affirming that tradition, he felt that there is no need to be overwhelmed with any degree of anxiety. With the same conviction regarding God's nearness and care St. Paul boldly asks, *"If God is for us, who can be against us…* (Romans 8:31—Today's English Version)?

Don't forget that Jesus knew God's nature, not only from his faith heritage, but also from his personal experience. His example has led me to the conviction that a heritage of faith sensitizes us to certain issues, but those issues increasingly become ours as we personally experience their validity. For example, my parents reared me in a particular faith tradition that placed considerable value upon cultivating a personal relationship with God the ultimate one to whom I would give my deepest loyalty. They also taught me to value the freedom derived from that relationship, including our freedom from bondage to sin on the one hand and bondage to one of sin's kissing cousins, restrictive religious legalism, on the other.

I was taught to value the leading of God that comes through the Holy Spirit who, Jesus said, was given as a gift from God to—among other things— guide us into all truth.

With regard to scripture and tradition I learned prayerfully to study them and, through a process of individual and group reflection, coupled with reason, to interpret and to value them.

In the process of growing in faith, personally experiencing the blessing of God's reality and God's deliverance from bondage to freedom, my feet are firmly planted on those realities, a platform from which I respond both to the opportunities and challenges of life.

But back to Jesus: think of the times when he and his family experienced the blessings of God's help, beginning with the way in which God led his parents, Joseph and Mary, away from the king's jealous determination to kill him:

> *"Now when they* (the Magi) *had departed, behold, an angel of the Lord appeared to Joseph in a dream and said, 'Rise, take the child and his mother, and flee to Egypt and remain there till I tell you; for Herod is about to search for the child to destroy him.' And he rose and took the child and his mother by night, and departed to Egypt, and remained until the death of Herod"* (Matthew 2:13-15—Today's English Version).

In his dynamic struggle with Satan on the Mount of Temptation, Jesus experienced the power from God that enabled him to resist the strongest kinds of temptation when in his most vulnerable state (Matthew 4:1-11, Mark 1:12-13, Luke 4:1-13). He emerged from this experience with a renewed, empowering alliance with God. He was ready to take on the world.

Throughout his ministry, Jesus felt the sustaining hand of God. On one occasion when he was showing his wannabe disciples that to follow him was not for the purpose of gaining material and political security, he declared, *"Foxes have holes, and birds of the air have nests, but the Son of Man has nowhere to lay his head* (Mathew 8:20—New Revised Standard Version). Yet, knowing the way in which God sustains, especially when our circumstances seem dismal, Jesus speaks with conviction this promise, *"… seek first his* (God's) *kingdom and his righteousness, and all these things* (the necessities of life) *shall be yours as well"* (Matthew 6:33—King James Version).

From his experience of God's protection and deliverance, Jesus knew that God would take care of his every need. Strengthened by his experience, he knew that he need not become the victim of anxiety. He was convinced that the power of God's loving commitment to him was much greater than the power of any anxiety.

Perhaps, as never before in his life, that conviction would be tested in the hours just prior to his arrest, trial and crucifixion. As he prayed in the Garden of Gethsemane the thick fog of anxiety moved in on him and, for a moment, appeared to have a chance at strangling him.

Listen to Luke's version of that experience:

"…he…knelt down and prayed, 'Father if thou art willing, remove this cup (of suffering) *from me; (now* listen for it!) *nevertheless not my will, but thine, be done.'* (Uh oh! anxiety must have exclaimed!) *And there appeared to him an angel from heaven, strengthening him. And being in agony he prayed more earnestly; and his sweat became like great drops of blood falling down upon the ground…."* (Luke 22:41-44—Revised Standard Version).

Though the scene depicts a time of extreme emotional distress, it also is careful to point out how God sustained Jesus by sending an angel to strengthen him and enable him to rise up from what momentarily appeared to be defeat to face boldly those who were at the garden's edge to arrest him, a boldness that expressed itself during the trials that night (Thursday) and his crucifixion the next day.

Throughout his life, Jesus knew God would take care of him. He learned of it in the heritage of faith from his ancestors but his conviction of its veracity would be confirmed and deepened in his own experience.

And if that were not enough, Jesus had a relationship with God which gave him a unique capacity to discern the presence and sustaining power of God. The Christian doctrine of Trinity— Father, Son, and Holy Spirit —symbolizes Jesus' oneness with God and the Spirit. He knew the mind and commitment better than any other human being.

In his *Letter to the Colossians*, the Apostle Paul references the depth and quality of that divine relationship:

> "*Christ is the **visible likeness** of the **invisible God**. He is the first born Son, superior to all created things. God created everything in heaven and on earth, the seen and the unseen things, including spiritual powers, lords, rulers, and authorities. God created the whole universe through him and for him.*
>
> *Christ existed before all things, and in union with him all things have their proper place. ....For it was by God's own decision that the Son has in himself the **full nature of God...**"* (Colossians 1:1:15—Today's English Version).

With profound eloquence Jesus declared, "*The Father and I are one*" (John 10:30—Revised Standard Version).

My point is that the unique relationship Jesus had with God gave him a special capacity for discerning God's care. Although he would face tremendous pressures throughout his life and especially in the closing days of his ministry, all of which possessed the threat of drowning him in a sea of anxiety, Jesus' experience of God's sustaining presence and loving guidance delivered him through it all.

Now here is the gist of the profound nature of his counsel: His faith heritage that taught of God's sustaining care, his personal experience of that care, and his unique relationship which enabled him to perceive and share the mind of God, were all at play when he looked with compassion upon his followers and said, *"Do not be anxious."*

How could he have drawn any other conclusion?! If God's love is at the center of our life and world, with a deep concern for and an unlimited power to deliver us, it seems absurd that he would take any other position than that which encourages us not to be anxious and not to worry.

Can *you* hear his *"Do not be anxious"* directly? Can you *believe* it? We will pursue that a bit later. For now let me say that to the extent we are able to comprehend Jesus' conviction that God is greater than any anxiety, we will be drawn to it and feel an inclination to embrace it for ourselves.

As we face the anxiety of living, how can we be open to the magnetism of God's love so that it grows to become a compelling force driving us into the sustaining arms of God?

Let's now move in the direction to which that question points.

Examining Our Own Experience

Moving to embrace Jesus' conviction that God is greater than our anxiety and that God invites us to embrace an experience of such Sovereign care is necessary if we are able to experience wholeness.

For many, however, experiencing and embracing a vision of God's care can become difficult. The potential for that difficulty challenges us to give it some consideration in the hope that folk experiencing it will be able to move through it to a life-giving experience of God's assurance.

Two primary factors contribute to the difficulty of the task: (1) Our natural inclination toward anxiety and (2) the pressure we feel from the nature of our times.

Natural Inclination: Our human nature invites large doses of anxiety. For some the anxiety may be rooted in the challenge of acquiring adequate food and shelter. But for most of us it seems rooted in the insecurity we feel with issues related to our employment, our economy, our relationships, and our health.

It's not unusual to hear: "I've got a job now, but I find myself questioning how long it will last." "The stock market is so volatile, I lie awake at night thinking about the vulnerability of my investments." "Sometimes I feel my relationships, particularly my primary ones, are weaker than I'd like them to be."

"How vulnerable am I to some of the devastating diseases that seem always to be attacking—cancer, Alzheimer, heart failure, diabetes and the like?"

We sense our own anxiety and often become curious about whether others are feeling the same. When in small gatherings where the trust level is high enough for individuals to be open with their feelings, we learn that so much of the anxiety we feel is being experienced by others as well. During such moments we may feel better about ourselves when we hear another say, "Yeah, I'm feeling the same things!" At least such disclosures help us to realize that we are not "lone rangers."

It does seem that there is something in our human nature, perhaps our desire to survive and succeed, that senses—and often magnifies—the forces that would block our success in achieving that outcome.

The Nature of our Times: Every generation of human beings has the burden of anxiety but the form and intensity of the anxiety experienced may vary with historical points in time. For example, Jesus first addressed his "don't worry or be anxious" message in the first century to the common people of Palestine most of whom were poor with small village or rural roots. Sensing their anxiety and feeling that it revolved around the issues of food, clothing and shelter, in his *Sermon on the Mount* he addresses those concerns. While there are millions today whose anxiety has similar roots, most of us—

particularly in Europe and North America—are relatively affluent.

In modern times we are made anxious by a wider scope of issues ranging from fear of being depersonalized (feeling that we're only a number or cog in a vast machine) to the challenge posed by the complexity of modern technology and the rapid pace of change. Sprinkled in between are other challenges such as the threat of terrorism and of nuclear holocaust, environmental deterioration, and the breakdown of family. Add to those our loss of touch and kinship with nature, the imperialism of sprawling urbanization, and materialism.

In short, I sense that while every generation has found it necessary to deal with ample insecurity and its resulting anxiety, the distinctive pressures of the 21st century have intensified long-standing anxiety sources and introduced new ones, a combination that places unprecedented pressure upon us.

I am suggesting, therefore, that these two factors—our natural inclination toward insecurity and the nature of our times—create considerable challenges for the task of dealing successfully with our worries.

Nevertheless, though it is not easy to deal with our insecurity and its attending anxiety, I believe it is not impossible. Why would Jesus encourage us not to worry or be anxious if such a state were impossible? That would be totally out of character for him.

However, in spite of the formidable challenges to dealing successfully with it, I believe we may be making management of our anxiety more difficult than it needs to be.

Why? Because we perceive those challenges simply from a *rational* perspective. For example, on the one hand, we can easily conclude that coping with such huge challenge seems, from a rational point of view, to be impossible. On the other hand, we may think that our challenges demand of us only a "decision" not to worry or be anxious, as though by use of some mental gymnastic we can clear the hurdle.

Simply from a *rational* point of view then, we fall into one of two traps— that of thinking the challenge to be impossible or that of underestimating what it demands of us. To meet the challenges of life successfully we must base our assessments of their difficulty and solution, not just on our *rational* faculty, but on other dimensions of our human capacity as well.

Consider that Jesus was prompted to offer his counsel not to worry or be anxious by his view that God makes available a provision of inspiration and power which creates for us the option of getting control of our lives. It is as though Jesus is saying to us, "Yes, the challenge to manage your worry and anxiety is huge, but there is a power available from deep in the care and strength of God that will give you aid." To those of us who feel that we need simply to buck up and decide to meet the challenge on our own, he may be saying, " It's not that simple! Don't assume that you can just *decide* not to be anxious." In either case he seems to be saying, "It's not just up to you. God is present and willing to help by strengthening the power of your decision and choice; thus reducing the size of what seems to be an impossible challenge."

In light of the divine promise, Jesus is encouraging us to open ourselves to God, receiving and trusting God's alliance in the challenge of overcoming worry and anxiety.

To make sure that even the simplest among us could trust that alliance, he declares in his sermon:

> *"This is why I tell you: do not be worried about the food and drink you need in order to stay alive, or about clothes for your body. After all, isn't life worth more than food? And isn't the body worth more than clothes? Look at the birds; they do not plant seeds, gather a harvest and put it in barns, yet your Father in heaven takes care of them! Aren't you worth much more than birds? Can any of you live a bit longer by worrying about it?*
>
> *And why worry about clothes? Look how the wild flowers grow; they do not work or make clothes for themselves. But I tell you that not even King Solomon with all his wealth had clothes as beautiful as one of these flowers. It is God who clothes the wild grass—grass that is here today and gone tomorrow…. Won't he be all the more sure to clothe you? What little faith you*

have. So do not start worrying; 'Where will my food come from? Or my drink? Or my clothes? ....Your Father in heaven knows that you need all these things. Instead, be concerned above everything else with the Kingdom of God and with what he requires of you, and he will provide you with all these other things. So do not worry about tomorrow; it will have enough the troubles each day brings" (Matthew 6:25-34 — Today's English Version).

Concentrating on Jesus' message helps us to realize that, while our rational factors are not to be *excluded* in developing a strategy for dealing with our anxiety, we need *more* than the power of our minds alone. We need also the power of our *spiritual dimension,* that part of us that enables us to expand our human potential by opening the gates of our minds and hearts to receive divine wisdom and power.

The human mind is an amazing phenomenon. With proper training it is able to grasp complex concepts in philosophy, mathematics, physics and chemistry. It is also capable of tracing history and making predictions about the future as well as to bathe in the richness of great literature and art. But when it comes to dealing with anxiety its limitations are immediately revealed.

In dealing with anxiety the mind becomes the patient that cannot heal itself, not that it is *impotent* but that it is *fragmented, diffused,* and *afflicted* to the point of not being able sufficiently to get its focus clear and its energy generated.

That's why we have to utilize the tools of the human spirit that come from a deeper dimension within us where we are equipped with spiritual ears that hear beyond our ordinary hearing and spiritual eyes to see beyond our ordinary seeing. With such expansion of our seeing and hearing we sense the presence of God who offers to enter into partnership with us. In that partnership, dealing with worry becomes not just a matter of the *brain* but also a matter of the *heart*; not just *me* versus the challenge, but *us*—God, others, and me—moving to conquer it.

Clearly, the confidence that enabled Jesus to call us beyond anxiety and worry comes from a God-centered world view that requires more than intellectual analysis and the strength of one's natural will. That "more" comes from the spiritual realm when and where our deepest selves begin to sense the presence of God's love. In that situation we begin to open up to and to trust that love in such a way that our will and passion for healing and wholeness begin to mesh with God's care. That process results in strength enough to win the war over anxiety or any other force that stands in the way of our becoming what God wants us to be.

Such meshing together of our need and God's love is not to be taken lightly. It is a process that requires considerable openness to God and trust in what God can do for and with us. And there is the rub.

Perhaps you are as aware as I that our spiritual "connectors" and "receptors" are often crusted over and dulled through lack of discipline and use. That dullness has to be taken seriously. If not, it may find us trying to plug into the power source with impaired and inadequate connectors.

Recently, when I was getting ready to trim the hedges that surround our house, I plugged in my cord, flipped the switch to "on" position, pressed the trigger and nothing happened. I soon discovered that the cord had been damaged, disabling it from transferring the current from my wall socket into the hedge trimmer.

Sometimes we experience a similar disconnect with God's love and power. In such cases it becomes imperative to do a review of our "connector(s)," a process designed to reveal that which is blocking the flow between ourselves and God. The blocking force(s) discovered may be multiple, but often they relate to shallowness or lack of discipline on our part. For example we may discover that our efforts to make the connection have consisted of utilizing only leftover fragments of time and concentration in spare moments while reserving most of our time and concentration to "larger" and "more important" projects.

In my youth, the expression I often heard to describe such approach to God was "half-hearted." Our Appalachian culture used that term when referring to inadequate commitment brought to a project, whether it had to do with a mundane challenge of accomplishing a job on the farm or to the project of deepening our relationship with God. We were taught that the "half-hearted" approach was simply not adequate for producing the divine chemistry between ourselves and God powerful enough to move mountains of insecurity, anxiety and worry.

While half-heartedness is not just a modern affliction—like anxiety it has been in humans of every generation—it seems more apparent in our time which constantly bombards us with forces that compete for our loyalty both to God and to one another. These forces which make a strong pitch for our loyalty become so appealing to our modern mind-set that they have the power to distract us from our relationship to God and to one another. Among them are our culture's vibrant secularism, materialism, consumerism, skepticism, and, yes, narcissism.

Like static on our old AM radios, these forces amplify their energy to preoccupy our minds and divide our loyalty thereby distorting any clear contemplation of our connection with God. As evidence that the line of communication between ourselves and God is not clear, we find, on closer examination, that we are, indeed, tossing to God only fragments of our time and concentration.

In face of this reality, it is not surprising that Jesus counsels all who seek God's freedom from the common, anxiety-producing insecurities of life to "... *Seek first his (God's) kingdom and his righteousness, all these things (things we need to live securely) will be yours as well*" (Matthew 6:33— Revised Standard Version).

Now, please, let's return to the main issue: How do we begin to escape the dilemma of powerlessness in order to deal successfully with the strong currents of anxiety which flow within us? I refresh your memory of my previous suggestion that there are multiple answers to that issue which include various types of therapies such as psychoanalysis, psychotherapy, group therapy, and pharmacological therapy (the use of prescription drugs).

Each of these and, on occasion, a combination of them can be effective in moving us forward. But the focus of this book is upon what I call *spiritual* therapy which comes through the discovery and utilization of spiritual dynamics for the purpose of healing. Jesus' work with people provides an excellent model of such therapy.

As we have seen, Jesus' world view was a Godcentered one in which he affirmed God presence and God's care for all creation as the central reality of existence. For him this central reality was the source of divine power made available to those who are *able* to receive it.

Please do not interpret this as an implication that God intends to make such power available only to a few people. That power is made available to everyone. But not everyone picks up on it or is able to utilize it. God's role is to make that sufficient power available to everyone, a role that God always plays perfectly. We humans have a role as well but unlike God, our performance is often spotty or fails completely. Spiritual therapy, as seen clearly in Jesus' work with people, is designed to improve our desire and ability to utilize God's power.

In light of our inadequacy I want to explore an extremely important issue with you, the issue at the heart of these questions: How can we improve our performance of appropriating and utilizing divine power in overcoming our difficulties with anxiety? How do we move beyond our propensity to spread our loyalties to many different forces around and within us while giving ourselves completely to none of them? How do we move from such meaningless diffusiveness (lack of specific focus) to an embrace of God's embrace?

These questions and their fundamental issue of commitment seemed always on Jesus' mind as he dealt with people during his earthly ministry. Now, as the risen Christ, he continues to consider them as he ministers to us in our own time. Because he experienced human existence fully, he knows that one of our greatest challenges is to overcome the existential dilemma of extreme difficulty in breaking free from our preoccupations with our own security—the root of our anxiety—to reach out to God.

Precisely, the question before is: What is Jesus' formula for enabling us to break this cycle of failure to connect with God's liberating power?

Jesus' Prescription for Our Difficulties

Our dilemma is knotty and complex. The prescription Jesus offers must possess a potency that can loosen the Gordian knot into which we humans have tightly woven ourselves.

As we are about to see, the prescription embodies more than calls for attitude adjustments, change of schedules, diets, and better preparation for sound sleep routines, important as all these are for our well-being. Full of divine knowledge, now complemented with his significant experience as a human being among other humans, Jesus seems convinced that anything short of complete reconstruction of humans will fail to deliver us from the steel-like grasp of our anxiety-producing insecurity. He is aware that this severe insecurity forces us to be intensely preoccupied with our own welfare. He is aware, too, that this preoccupation is strengthened by a sense of paranoia that causes us to view God, one another, and nature through spectacles of suspicion which makes them appear as contestants—even enemies—which must be manipulated and overcome in an effort to establish our own security.

Therefore, any reconstruction must be thorough enough to reach into our center and break the hold of self-preoccupation.

What is needed, Jesus concludes, is re-creation capable of producing a *new* person. He speaks of being born *again*, with this second birth being *spiritual* in contrast to our original *physical* one.

As I approach this subject I am aware that we are about to walk upon very delicate ground. At least two issues make it delicate. *First,* a concept of spiritual rebirth is strange for our culture so steeped in secularism, materialism and skepticism, any one of which has the power to close the gates leading to spirituality. *Secondly,* within some religious communities significant distortion and/or trivialization of the noble concept has occurred leaving an odor of confusion both for some within these communities and among many outside observers.

With these in mind, I approach the subject of spiritual birth with sharper awareness and sensitivity than earlier in my life. For example, regarding the nature of our culture, I am increasingly convinced that in order to be effective, any talk of spiritual rebirth with persons who are steeped in the "isms" referenced above must be sensitive to their *suspicion* of spiritual issues. At the same time the conversation needs awareness of their deep hunger for meaning along with their disappointment that their particular "ism" has not been able to deliver it to them.

With regard to the second issue—that of distortion and trivialization of spiritual birth within religious communities—I experience two growing realizations, (1) that in order to be widely influential our talk of spiritual birth needs to make clear that no one group has a monopoly on this wonderful gift of God to the world (as though it cannot be experienced by faithful seekers in other groups or Faiths), and (2) to resist the cheapening distortion that followers of Christ are divided into two categories—those "born again" and those not born again (as though the Body of Christ [the Church] is made up of *first* and *second* class citizens).

At a time when Christianity has become so institutionalized, I am increasingly compelled to see God and God's provisions for creation as much larger than the institutionalized church and faith to be much deeper than commitment to belief systems.[1]

With regard to those who would divide Christ's followers into those born again and those not born again, I remember that Jesus made no such distinction.

His point in discussing the new or spiritual birth is that such an experience is necessary for anyone who is able to escape the vicious cycle of insecurity with its devastating worry and anxiety.

With that said, I invite you to join me as we open ourselves to the story in which Jesus speaks of being born again:

"There was a Jewish leader named Nicodemus, who belonged to the party of the Pharisees. One night he went to Jesus and said to him, 'Rabbi, we know that

you are a teacher sent by God. No one could perform the miracles you are doing unless God were with him.'

Jesus answered, 'I am telling you the truth, no one can see the Kingdom of God without being born again.'

'How can a grown man be born again?' Nicodemus asked. He certainly cannot enter his mother's womb and be born a second time!' 'I am telling you the truth,' replied Jesus, 'that no one can enter the Kingdom of God without being born of water and the Spirit. A person is born physically of human parents, but is born spiritually of the Spirit"

'How can this be?' asked Nicodemus.

Jesus answered, 'You are a great teacher in Israel, and you don't know this?'" (John 3:1- 8 —Today's English Version).

What a story! In face of it you may be as puzzled as Nicodemus.

"What is Jesus talking about?" you may be asking.

Let's examine the conversation more closely. Jesus' response to Nicodemus, *"You are a great teacher in Israel, and you don't know this?"* infers that this spiritual, or second birth, lies deep within the Jewish tradition and should be known by anyone in Nicodemus' position.

Jesus, therefore, in his talk about new birth, seems not to be implying a brand new concept. Rather, I see him buffing, polishing, and re-imaging an existing one to which he is giving new emphasis with fresh nuances of meaning. The re-imaging metaphor is that of new birth—God's way of creating us anew or reconstructing us from the ground up. The thought is that our old being, in bondage to powerful forces, is breaking forth into a new being empowered by the dynamic power of God's Spirit.

Had not scores of God's faithful down through the centuries of Hebrew history experienced divine transformation with the result that they became capable of coping successfully with the challenges of life and of serving God faithfully?

First century societies were very religious not only in Israel but beyond (See St. Paul's comments in Acts 17:16-31 regarding the prevalence of religion). But its power to transform life and give it meaning had sunk to a new low. (Some believe a similar situation has occurred among religious folk in our own time.) In face of such religious impotence, Jesus speaks as though it is time for a *revival* as a way of restoring a dynamic faith which has morphed into institutionalized religiosity.

I believe that as Jesus declared it to his first century audience, he declares it to us: It's time for us to open ourselves to God in such a way that our stagnant ceremonies give way to the fresh waters of dynamic faith strong enough to transform our *self-preoccupation* into *compassion,* freeing us not only to celebrate for *ourselves* but to draw *others* into the celebration.

For those of us who may be religious, I think it is not as though Jesus is calling us to abandon authentic religious beliefs and practices. Rather I hear him calling us to realize that it's time to utilize our religious forms (beliefs, ways of worship and serving) not as ends in themselves but as means designed to usher us into a renewed experience of God's love and grace, its power to free us from those things that block us from God, from one another, and from constructive service throughout creation.

Jesus appears to desire, for Nicodemus and us, an awareness that we can live on a far higher plane than the one available through mere religiosity. He wants to instill in us an awareness of the transforming power of God available to us, so dynamic that to experience it is like being born anew.

In that "rebirthing" process we discover we are no longer the old persons of selfish preoccupation with its suspicion and distrust. We begin to experience ourselves as new persons in whom compassion and trust reign. Such radical transformation at the core of our being reflects nothing short of being born again.

If my hunch is correct that, in speaking of spiritual birth, or being born again, Jesus is putting fresh emphasis upon a concept deep in the faith tradition of Israel. I ask you: Could it be that it was such an experience that *Moses* had at the burning bush in the land of Midian (Exodus 3), or *David,* following his repentance of sinning with Bathsheba and the death of their son (1 Kings 12), or *Isaiah,* following his vision of and conversation with God in the Holy Temple (Isaiah 6:1-8)? Could these stories of their transforming experiences of faith be similar to, if not actual reflections of, what Jesus is presenting to Nicodemus and to us?

All these incidents—and many others—are visible, through the scripture and tradition of Israel to which Nicodemus had access. As an educated leader in Israel, he should have known about the process of spiritual sensitivity which discerns and embraces the coming of God's Spirit into a life, freeing and empowering it to accomplish magnificent things. Could it be that Nicodemus' failure to connect the dots is indicative of the low point to which the Israel's religious establishment had arrived in the first century? Over time doesn't every major religious movement experience that cycle?

By suggesting that Jesus is describing a longstanding experience in Judaism, it is not my aim to minimize the effect of his new birth teaching. Part of his messianic role is not only to *make clear* that God will, at all times, bring deep spiritual rebirth on the heels of authentic repentance in order to free people but also to *inspire* and *empower* that repentance.

I'm convinced that Jesus did this, not only with his verbal teaching—as in his conversation with Nicodemus—but also by the drama of his "Son of God" ministry, climaxing in his death and resurrection, all of which made him a cosmic magnet capable of pulling us and all creation toward God (John 12:32).

Now consider this: Jesus' metaphor "being born again" (John 3:3) implies, as in the case of physical birth, an intimate moment of "impregnation" in which a new being begins formation. That "seminal" moment in preparation for being born again is that point at which a person arrives at genuine faith, not faith as a *belief system*, but faith (in its basic biblical sense) as *trusting God* so completely that we leap into God's arms, surrendering our wills to God's. There in the warmth and inspiration of God's accepting embrace, we discover and rejoice in the freedom from our former bondage. In that embrace we become aware that our hearts, once filled with self-preoccupation, are turning outward with compassion. Happily, we enter into a covenant with God to serve God's purposes in the world and its peoples.

An experience available to every one, this new life becomes an experienced reality in those who see in the lives of the faithful—especially in the life of Jesus –what God is really like. As a result many "beholders" are drawn by that magnificent vision to trust God so deeply that they are willing to take what some have called a "the leap of faith."

"Don't worry or be anxious" may sound impractical, even impossible, to those who limit their resources exclusively to mind and will. But for those who sense the availability of God's Spirit and open themselves to receive and trust the power the

Spirit brings into their lives, Jesus' admonition not to be anxious does not seem either impractical or impossible.

Indeed, I think it was for such an experience that Jesus came among us. Indeed, he declares it: *"I came that they may have life, and have it **abundantly**"* (John 10:10—Revised Standard Version). The deep quality of that abundant life is underscored in another remarkable statement by Jesus*: "I am telling you the truth those who hear my words and believe in him who sent me **have eternal life**. They will not be judged, but **have already passed from death to life**"* (John 5:24—Today's English Version).

This abundant life, infused with a present experience of eternity is far better than our ordinary natural life. Jesus' imagery of new birth points to the ability, by the power of God, to shape our lives more in line with God's original design for us. The contrast between natural living and spiritual living is such that our situation moves from the column of ordinary life to that of abundant life; from earth and time-bound existence to eternal life.

Listen to the security and freedom for the faithful underlined in these telling passages of scripture:

> *"My sheep listen to my voice; I know them, and they follow me. I give them eternal life, and they shall never die. No one can snatch them from me* (From Jesus in John 10:2728—Today's English Version).

"…you belong to God, my children, and have defeated the false prophets, because the Spirit who is in you is more powerful than the spirit in those who belong to the world" (1 John 4:4—Today's English Version).

"I can do all things through Christ who strengthens me" (Philippians 4:13—Revised Standard Version).

Or, as rendered in Today's English Version, *"I have the strength to face all conditions by the power Christ gives me."*

Do you catch it? Does the promise catch you? We can be rescued from being *victims* of life's anxiety. We can be reborn as *victors* through the discovery and utilization of the spiritual power God makes available to us through the Spirit, the power that is able to transform our inordinate self-orientation (the seat of our anxiety) into compassion (the sign of freedom from our anxiety) !

Hear this clearly: It is not necessary that we drown in the sea of anxiety so deep and wide in human experience! That good news of the Gospel prompted one biblical writer to exclaim, *"…you belong to God, my children, and have defeated the false prophets, because the Spirit who is in you is more powerful than the spirit in those who belong to the world"* (I John 4:4—Today's English Version).

At this writing I am late into my seventh decade. When I reflect on my longevity I am amazed that the years have come and gone so quickly. "It seems only yesterday that…" has become a regular response as I review the journey on which I continue.

Daily thanksgiving flows from my heart for my continuing vigor and health. Aware of having entered the world of elderly, I still dream of new chapters in my experience of this young century. At the same time I am increasingly conscious of my mortality; that one day I shall experience physical death. However, even death does not feel like the end for the precious gift of life that, years ago, I gave back to the Giver with the promise that through the Giver's shared strength I will be faithful throughout the journey.

Oh, there have been ups and downs, times of scarcity, times of anxiety and dread but like sniffles that congest us only for a while, I experience these as temporary inconveniences; never as slave masters. Always, I anticipate their passing and a fresh realization of the joyful experience of *belonging to* the loving heart of God and *serving in* God's divine corps. For me, that arrangement is continuously therapeutic and life giving!

At this very moment I can hear the reassuring song I sang as a child in worship, one that has blessed each chapter of my life. Titled, "His Eye Is on the Sparrow," it was inspired by the passage in which Jesus explains why he encourages us not to

worry and be anxious. Please meditate with me upon the song's
words:

> *Why should I feel discouraged—Why should*
> *the shadows come Why should my heart*
> *be lonely—and long for heaven & home*
> *when Jesus is my portion? My constant*
> *friend is he—His eye is on the sparrow*
> *and I know he watches me—His eye is on*
> *the sparrow and I know he watches me.*
>
> *Refrain: I sing because I'm happy—I sing*
> *because I'm free, for his eye is on the*
> *sparrow and I know he watches me.*
>
> *'Let not your heart be troubled"—*
> *his tender word I hear though by the*
> *paths he leadeth—but one step I may*
> *see: his eye is on the sparrow, and I*
> *know he watches me his eye is on the*
> *sparrow, and I know he watches me.*
>
> *Whenever I am tempted—whenever clouds*
> *arise—when song gives place to sighing,*
> *when hope within me dies, I draw close to*
> *him, from care he sets me free—his eye is*
> *on the sparrow and I know he watches me*

Words: Civilla D. Martin, 1905;

Music: Charles H. Gabriel, 1905

Faith connects us to an experience of God's love for all creation. It also joins us to an experience of God's commitment to empower and enable all creation to overcome those forces that seek to thwart its beauty and purpose.

It's nothing short of an experience of God's divine therapy!

Is it any wonder, then, that Jesus counsels us not to worry and be anxious? St. Paul, one of the most exciting of the apostles and the New Testament's most prolific writer, caught Jesus' spirit well. Out of that experience, he penned one of this most exciting messages of encouragement to anyone facing the strong challenges of life:

> *"Don't worry about anything, but in*
> *all your prayers ask God what what*
> *you need, always asking him with a*
> *thankful heart. And God's peace, which*
> *is far beyond human understanding,*
> *will keep your hearts and minds safe*
> *in union with Christ Jesus"* (Philippians
> 4:6-7—Today's English Version).

Oh, how precious is the victory won through our trust in God's love made so visible in Jesus! Insecurity and anxiety are not gods. God is God! And God has broken the tyranny, liberating us from anything that aims to thwart our destiny.

Moreover, God accompanies us on a fulfilling compassionate journey of building a better world.

That freedom *from* is an important side of a larger equation designed to deliver us. We are set free *for* something as well—to join with God and others in purposeful and compassionate work in the world. That work, like our faith in God, is remarkably therapeutic in delivering us from anxiety's grasp. It contributes mightily to breaking our pattern of self obsession by its call to focus compassionately upon the needs of other human beings and the wide arena of nature.

Let us now turn to a consideration of some specific forms that work may take, what it looks like.

CHAPTER THREE

Faith Connects Us to the World (Therapeutic Work)

"He who labors as he prays lifts his heart to God with his hands."

St. Bernard of Clairvaux

"God likes help in helping people."

Irish Proverb

Freedom From and Freedom For

Being set free from our enslavement to worry and anxiety is not an end in itself. It's a step in a process of becoming healthy participants in building a better world. Faith—understood in the biblical sense—is not only a "get out of jail" card. It's also an invitation to share in the work of God to correct self-imposed distortions in creation as a step in moving toward its divinely intended destiny. In other words, *faith* (trust) in God sets us free for the *work* of God. Faith and work are two sides of the came coin.

Something happens in the process of our deliverance from destructive anxiety that changes our primary focus from the individual self—which is the initial problem—to a wider experience of engagement with the others who, like us, have been liberated for the common good. In this refreshed view others no longer look like adversaries and competitors for, through the chemistry of spiritual transformation, they appear as our brothers and sisters joined to us in an amazing new pilgrimage.

In other words, this community of the liberated is now set free to hook up with one another and with God in a joint effort to build a better world. We have a new and compelling vision which promises to lead to the ultimate defeat of the enslaving powers.

Our freedom, then, has a *direction* and a *purpose*. Its direction is away from self-preoccupation and toward the common good. Its purpose is to partner with God (please see 2 Corinthians 6:1) in building the kind of world for which Jesus teaches us to pray, "*...Thy kingdom come; Thy will be done on earth as it is in heaven....*"

Because preoccupation with the self is the source of that which dwarfs and distorts us we must avoid any hint that

God's deliverance is primarily for the *self.* This point seems uppermost in Jesus' mind as he declares: "*Those who try to gain their own life will lose it; but those who lose their life for my sake will gain it*" (Matthew 10:38-39—Today's English Version).

Jesus exemplifies the truth of which he speaks, namely, that wholeness and meaning come through our surrender of the self for a larger cause.

This is not exclusively a theological insight. It is affirmed in modern psychology as well. For example, Victor Frankl, the Viennese psychiatrist, in his book, *Man's Search For Ultimate Meaning,* writes:

"…man (sic) is originally characterized by his 'search for meaning' rather than his 'search for himself.' The more he forgets himself—giving himself to a cause or another person— the more human he is. And the more he is immersed and absorbed in something or someone other than himself the more he really becomes himself." [1]

Following his instruction for a major chore on the farm, my dad used to say to my brother and me, "Boys, I know it's going to demand some sweat, but remember that good hard work for the cause of family harms no one. In fact it takes care of a lot of stress while keeping you out of trouble and putting food on the table. Now you can't beat that deal!"

The point is that in the biblical tradition, faith is always a two-sided experience of being set free *from* something and, at the same time, *for* something.

This insight is of crucial importance in our journey toward wholeness. Ours is a freedom from too much emphasis upon the self in order to focus upon something larger. It represents more, therefore, than repainting an old clunker which remains the same old clunker with a new look. It represents a complete reconstruction that produces something new.

St. Paul puts it this way: *"Anyone who is joined to Christ is a new being, the old is gone, the new has come. All this is done by God, who through Christ changed us from enemies into his friends and gave us the task of making others his friends also"* (2 Corinthians 5:17-18—Today's English Version).

Multiple examples of this concept of freedom for something larger are given in both the Old and New Testaments of the Bible. Let's take a moment to look at an example from each of those biblical sections:

Isaiah's Story

Isaiah was called to be a prophet to Judah in the early 700's B.C. The story of his call marks a dramatic moment in his life. This encounter with God will change him forever and will serve subsequent generations as a model of that which comes with an authentic experience of God's liberation from self preoccupation.

The setting for the prophet's experience is the Temple in Jerusalem. Listen to his report:

"…I saw the Lord. He was sitting on his throne, high and exalted, and his robe filled the whole Temple. Around him flaming creatures were standing.…They were calling out to each other: 'Holy, holy, holy! The Lord God

Almighty is holy! His glory fills the world.'

The sound of their voices made the foundation of the Temple shake, and the Temple itself became filled with smoke.

I said, 'There is no hope for me! I am doomed because every word that passes my lips is sinful; and I live among a people whose every word is sinful. And yet, with my own eyes I have seen the King, the Lord Almighty'

Then one of the creatures flew down to me, carrying a burning coal that he had taken from the altar with a pair of tongs. He touched my lips with the burning coal and said, 'This has touched your lips, and now your guilt is gone, and your sins are forgiven.'" (Isaiah 6:1-2a, 3-7—Today's English Version).

Isaiah is so deeply affected by this experience of God's holy presence that he begins to reflect upon his own condition. So moved is he by his own sinfulness, as well as that of others in

Judah, he confesses his unworthiness. God does not reject but renews him by sending an angel with a hot coal from the altar to touch his lips and make him clean: *"This has touched your lips, and now your guilt is gone and your sins are forgiven"* (verse 7).

In response, what will Isaiah do? Will he gather some of his friends, go out to lunch, and describe this amazing experience? Will he wear this experience as a badge of honor with which to impress others? Will his experience with God become an end in itself?

The answer is "No!" In the very next verse Isaiah reports an immediate challenge from God: *"Then I heard the Lord say, 'Whom shall I send? Who will be our messenger?'* to which Isaiah responds, *"I will go! Send me!"*

Do you see it? Have you experienced this in your own life? When the Lord liberates us from the troublesome anxiety of self preoccupation we are challenged with "Step Two," that of committing ourselves to work alongside God for improvement of God's precious world. That move continues the therapeutic process of freeing us from anxiety by helping take our eyes off inordinate self-concern through involvement in something other than and larger than ourselves.

Isaiah's story reminds us that when we respond positively to God's invitation to join the work to which God is calling us, we are involved in a process that is genuinely transforming.

The Story of Paul and Silas

There is this very interesting story about the Apostle Paul and one of his colleagues, Silas. They are well to the northwest of Israel, in the province of Macedonia, spreading the news of the Gospel and inviting people to become followers of Jesus. Their journey brings them to the city of Philippi. There an incident occurs which, like that of Isaiah, teaches us about the commitment that continues the process of our spiritual liberation.

The two have been arrested, beaten and thrown into the city jail's innermost cell where they have been bound by chains. The experience that follows is anything but ordinary. We are told that about midnight they began to pray and to sing hymns to God. Luke, the story's writer, adds, "*… the other prisoners were listening to them.*"

Then all heaven breaks loose! Listen as Luke continues:

> *"Suddenly there was a violent earthquake, which shook the prison to its foundations. At once all the doors opened, and the chains fell off all the prisoners. The jailer woke up, and when he saw the prison doors open, he thought that the prisoners had escaped; so he pulled out his sword and was about to kill himself* (Better suicide than the wrath of his superiors!!). *But Paul shouted at the top of his voice, 'Don't harm yourself. We are all here!'*

> *The jailer called for a light, rushed in, and fell trembling at the feet of Paul and Silas. Then he led them out and asked, 'Sirs, what must I do to be saved?'*
>
> *They answered, 'Believe in the Lord Jesus, and you will be saved—you and your family.' Then they preached the word of the Lord to him and to all the others in the house.*
>
> *At that very hour of the night the jailer took them and washed their wounds and he and all his family were baptized at once. Then he took Paul and Silas up into his house and gave them some food to eat. He and his family were filled with joy, because they now believed in God"* (Acts 16:25-34—Today's English Version).

The intervention of God which liberates Paul and Silas re-enforces our faith that God has an eye on us at all times, looking out for us under all circumstances. But the story proceeds to illustrate the concept that the freedom God brings to us is not just freedom from something. It is, at the same time, freedom for something. In this case the Apostle and his cohort are freed to rescue the jailer from suicide and to become catalysts for the dramatic conversion of his family.

Under similar circumstances wouldn't we be as excited as Paul and Silas? There is joy in doing that for which we are set free—committing ourselves to be co-workers with God for the betterment of society. As in their case, our participation in God's work *continues a process of liberation* from the prison of self-preoccupation. In other words, the moment of liberation is both an initial experience with God and a continuing experience as we become co-workers with God in renewing creation. I heard one person put it this way, "After our baptism, God never hangs us on the wall to dry! Salvation is not a trophy simply to be displayed."

The point is that both Isaiah's story and that of Paul and Silas make clear the integral connection between liberation from enslavement and freedom to join God's work. They remind us that our professed faith in God is made complete when it responds to the needs with which we are always surrounded.

If we allow our spiritual journey to stop short of joining in God's compassionate work toward others, it becomes a delusion that insures our perpetual bondage to the never-ceasing anxiety project of continuously endeavoring to establish our own security. A prime example of that delusion is the lady who complained to her pastor, "I get so much out of Jesus! I want to escape to him! I love *him* very much but I can't stand *people!*"

Self-preoccupation is so strong that it sometimes shortcuts an authentic experience of conversion with the poisonous notion that we can collect God as a trophy and just add that to our list of what makes us feel good and secure. Such a delusion reveals the extent to which our self-preoccupation turns us into giant sucking whirlpools that attempt to pull everything and everyone, including God, into ourselves.

Genuine conversion, however, experiences a moment of "Here am I, send me." It bows us before God to offer ourselves to God and God's compassionate pursuit of a better world in which all creation is enabled to enjoy the balance and harmony designed by God for abundant living. The faith that produces such results becomes very good therapy not only for our own souls but for the souls of humankind and, indeed, all creation.

The absence of this actively compassionate characteristic of authentic faith is the reason for the serious prophetic indictment brought upon Israel at a time when many of its folk were religious only for themselves. They expressed active religious observance while, at the same time, supporting and participating in widespread exploitation of the poor and the otherwise disenfranchised people in their midst. Ostensibly, they were worshiping God, praising God for deliverance, while simultaneously exploiting others, a sure sign that they were still strapped to the treadmill of attempting to secure their own existence.

The prophets considered this a serious distortion of the faith; indeed, a contradiction. Consider, for example, the following statements from Amos and Micah:

Reflect upon this passage from Amos:

*"Even though you offer me your burnt
offerings and grain offerings, I will not
accept them; and the offerings of wellbeing
of your fatted animals I will not
look upon. Take away from me the noise
of your songs; I will not listen to the
melody of your harps. But let justice roll
down like waters, and righteousness
like an everflowing stream"* (Amos 5:21-
24—New Revised Standard Version).

Micah follows with this:

*"He has told you, O mortal, what is good;
and what does the Lord require of you
but to do justice, and love kindness, and
to walk humbly with your God"* (Micah
6:8—New Revised Standard Version).

These two provide us a blazing reminder of the connection
between our *worship* (vertical faith) and our *work* (horizontal
faith). Their message is clear: We are liberated—or saved—for
a purpose and that purpose is to work with God to free God's
creation (all of it) from enslaving forces and to deliver it (all of
it) to its divinely intended destiny of peaceful harmony.

In the prayer he taught us, Jesus offers this descriptive of that destiny— "...*Thy will be done on **earth** as it is in **heaven**.*" I perceive Jesus' prayer as a call for all of us to join with God in the work that will make earth's situation the same as that in heaven as the two move in closer proximity until they have become one.

Apparently in the same vein of reflection John, in the New Testament book of *Revelation*, envisions heaven's coming down to earth in such a way that they are joined in everlasting unity and peace:

> "*Then I saw a new heaven and a new earth. The first heaven and the first earth disappeared, and the sea vanished. And I saw the Holy City, the new Jerusalem, coming down out of heaven from God, prepared and ready, like a bride dressed to meet her husband. I heard a loud voice speaking from the throne: 'Now God's home is with people! He will live with them, and they shall be his people. God himself will be with them, and he will be their God. He will wipe way all tears from their eyes. There will be no more grief or crying or pain. The old things have disappeared.' ....I did not see a temple in the city, because its temple is the Lord God Almighty and the Lamb. The city has no need of the sun or the moon to shine it it, because the glory of God shines on it, and the Lamb is its lamp. The peoples of*

the world will walk by its light…." (Revelation 21:1-4, 22-24a—Today's English Version).

Like the prayer of Jesus, this passage leans into the promise that God's creation will ultimately be rescued; that all its distortion will be transformed into perfection, harmony, and wholeness.

Do we understand just how that is to happen? No, the specific design behind the accomplishment is not made clear. It remains a part of the mystery of God. The faithful are invited to behold the vision and to trust it even if our *rationality* cannot fully grasp it. It's as though we are being asked to trust God enough to join the Divine in working toward a better world and to trust God's promise that the results of such Divine/human endeavor, while remaining mysterious for the moment, has the power to replace our self-preoccupation with a grand vision of world redemption which fills us with exhilarating hope.

Engaging with that process, we become aware that we are being liberated from our self-made prison and are swimming in the refreshing waters of freedom with a sense of purpose and destiny that provides us with hope, meaning and peace. Before the liberation, we were stuck in the mud of self-preoccupation. Now, with the transformation of our entire being, we realize that such selfishness has been replaced with a spirit of compassion that thrusts us into joining God in building a better world.

Trusting God and God's plan we are now ready to turn onto the home stretch in which we explore the specific character of that work and commit ourselves to joining with God and others in doing it.

The Character of Our Work

What does this work look like? It's not as though we have to speculate about the issue. Through the unfolding chapters of our Judeo-Christian heritage there are strong clues pointing to its character. Four categories have emerged in the Community of Faith around which there is considerable consensus:

Compassion for *Doing Justice*

Compassion for *Making Peace*

Compassion for *Practicing Conservation*

Compassion for *Sharing the Gospel's Good News*

A closer examination of each of these reveals that their roots lie deep in the Judeo-Christian tradition. The examination also shows that these categories of work enjoy considerable affirmation in the wider culture among spiritually sensitive persons, many of whom see themselves as standing outside any particular faith tradition.

With that, let's proceed to look more closely at each:

Compassion for *Doing Justice*

Doing justice begins with analyzing the "surroundings" of our culture in search of things that abuse not just human beings but other entities and systems in the world of nature as well. The process searches both for the abused and the abusers. When injustices are found "justice doers" commit themselves to the task of correcting them in such a way that, insofar as possible, they do not get repeated in the future.

When I engage in such reflection my mind races back to the days when my best friend and I would take a different bus to a different school each weekday morning. Pete, an African American, would board an old broken-down bus and travel to a wood frame school facility hemmed in with a fence and a dusty road, while I, an Anglo American, boarded a much nicer bus and proceeded to an elegant brick school building surrounded with beautiful landscaping. There was disparity not only in the vehicles and the school facilities, but in the quality of education received and the number of opportunity channels for continuing education and upward mobility.

At the time I recognized some of the differences. I remember feeling some discomfort and confusion. Only later would I affix the term "injustice" to the situation. It was then that I began to work toward correcting them.

Does your own reflection provide you with similar situations? Can you identify justice issues to which you are sensitive? Certainly, they surround us.

Think of widespread poverty and homelessness as they manifest themselves in urban centers here in the United States of America. Think, also, of thousands of refugees—particularly in the Middle East and parts of Africa —who have been displaced from their homes and villages now to languish in sprawling refugee camps, often without adequate food, water, and shelter from extreme heat or cold.

Consider those areas of the world where people are being persecuted because of their religious faith; places where both Christians and Muslims as well as persons of other religious groups are targeted for abuse.

Call to mind the thousands of immigrants who, surrounded by a society resistant to revising its immigration policies to provide genuine pathways to security, hunker down in the shadows with little hope.

Think of the great numbers of persons barred from the blessings of marriage because their conjugal relationship is with a person of the same gender.

More widely, consider the harm done to nature by all kinds of human activity that results in pollution of land, water, and air.

We are surrounded by injustices which have become virtual prisons for millions who yearn for equality, freedom, happiness and meaning. The victims are people and other natural entities created by God. The people are our brothers and sisters.

Wider nature is our kin as well.

In face of these and other reflections of injustice what shall we do? Shall we continue longheld rationalizations that give us a false sense of justification for resisting the work of doing justice? We hear it all around us, and sometimes within us… "Well, they're poor because they won't work for a living.…" "They've gotten themselves into a jam because they have broken the law.…" "There are always evil people who do evil things to others. It's always been that way and probably always will be.…" It goes on and on—easy rationalizations by which we seek to justify our apathy and inaction. But it is not in our divinely transformed nature to stand by and let injustice imprison so many. God is compassionate and has freed us to be compassionate as well. Therefore, we are at our very best when we find and utilize handles by which we can respond to the victims, handles that enable us to do justice in removing the circumstances that hold people down.

Doing the work of justice, we stand up for victims of injustice through constructive demonstrations of our compassion. This includes such things as writing checks to support just causes, making phone calls, sending e-mails, joining in public protests, and working for just legislation and policies, all aimed at setting aright those things that offend and abuse that which deserves our support.

When the prophet Amos approached the powers of his day, he delivered a scathing indictment of their insensitivity to and abuse of the poor and disenfranchised. Because these powers usually had a distinctly religious orientation, the prophet underscored the conflict between their professed religious values and their insensitivity to social injustice. He interpreted to them God's utter disgust with their continuing commitment to such contradiction.

Amos courageously and clearly articulated his recommendation to them: "…*let justice roll down like waters, and righteousness like an everflowing stream*" (Amos 5:14—Revised Standard Version).

That prophetic exhortation continues effectively to challenge people of faith—as well as others who value the concept of dignity—to reflect compassion for victims of social injustice by taking action to right those things that are clearly wrong.

At some point each of us has acted to correct an injustice. I suspect that some of you were active in the civil rights movement for which Dr. Martin Luther King, Jr. had such passion. Or it could be a setting in which, witnessing the pain of an injustice, you made—or are making—a stand which calls for a different approach.

Motivated by compassion, when we respond positively to the vision of justice, we are clearer about the reality and power of doing right. The adventure of doing justice has tremendous power to break the grip of self-obsession and set us free to enter into the adventure of caring for others.

Let us continue to be inspired to action as heed that ancient admonition:

"Let justice roll down like waters, and
righteousness like an everflowing stream."

Compassion for *Making Peace*

Daily newscasts have the potential of convincing us that the human race is destined to cannibalize itself. The warring spirit manifests itself on military battlefields, in incidents of terrorism, in the clash between lawbreakers and law keepers, and even in homes—anywhere human beings set themselves against one another in violent ways.

Many individuals are walking among us who are at war within themselves, a war that may eventually erupt with terrible consequences. For example, this morning's paper carried continuing news of a young father in our community whose inner conflict broke open into the violent shooting of his wife, one of her close friends, and the pastor of his church.

Against the background of this dismal and fractured picture, biblical faith lifts an alternative vision, that of persons at peace with themselves living in peace with others and working for the extension of peace everywhere.

For example, when the prophet Isaiah was inspired by a vision of the Messiah he wrote:

"The royal line of David is like a tree that has been cut down; but just as new branches sprout from a stump, so a new king will arise from among David's descendants.

The spirit of the Lord will give him wisdom and the knowledge and skill to rule his people. He will know the Lord's will and will honor him, and find pleasure in obeying him. He will not judge by appearance or hearsay; he will judge the poor fairly and defend the rights of the helpless. At his command nothing harmful or evil. The land will be as full of the knowledge of the Lord as the seas are full of water" (Isaiah 11:1-9— Today's English Version).

Isaiah's messianic faith enables him to challenge the worldly practice of warfare with an alternative. He envisions a time when all forms of violent competition among humans, between humans and animals, and among the animals themselves will have given way to peace.

Leap forward a few centuries to the coming of Jesus who, for Christians, is the fulfillment of the messianic prophecies. He is hailed as the Prince of Peace through whom a compelling vision of peacemaking will be acted out in the drama of his ministry.

In his Sermon on the Mount, Jesus declares: "*Happy are those who work for peace: God will call them his children*" (Matthew 5:9—Today's English Version).

Following his three year ministry during which he was a supreme example of peacemaking, he recognized that he was standing under the shadow of a cross. Among the several departing words to the disciples were these: "*Peace I leave with you, my peace I give to you. I do not give to you as the world gives. Do not let your hearts be troubled, and do not let them be afraid*" (John 14:27—New Revised Standard Version).

Jesus was and is all about peace and peacemaking. With the goal of working with God to drive the waring spirit out of all creation, He calls persons everywhere to share that passion.

Your and my peacemaking begins within. In his book, *Seeking Peace,* Johann Christoph Arnold reminds us that before we can make peace with others and with the world, we must make peace with ourselves.

In the preface to Arnold's work, Thjieh Nhat Hanh writes,

> "If we are at war with our parents, our family, our society or our church, there is probably a war going on inside us also. Therefore the most basic work for peace is to return to ourselves and create harmony among the elements within us—our feelings, our perceptions, our mental states." [2]

Sometimes we may think that working for peace has to do exclusively with getting rid of weapons, helping warring groups and nations find peaceful avenues for resolving their differences. Peacemaking is all that but it's more than that.

Jesus saw that the root of evil is in our hearts.

On one occasion he said,

> *"It is written, 'Thou shalt not kill, and whoever shall kill shall be in danger of judgment.' But I say unto you, that whosoever is angry with his brother without cause shall be in danger of the judgment…. Whosoever shall say, 'Thou fool,' shall be in danger of hell fire"* (Matthew 5:22—King James Version)

I take this to mean that peacemaking begins with uprooting war from ourselves and from the hearts of all men and women. Therefore, when Jesus declares to us, *"Peace I give unto you…,"* I believe he is addressing the root challenge of peacemaking, a revolution for peace within human beings who, in turn, proceed to pass that good germ to others in such a way that, ultimately, all human beings and their institutions become immune to warfare and violence.

In our own time—perhaps in all periods of history—the need for peace cries out. Listen again to Arnold,

"The need for peace cries to heaven. It is one of the deepest longings of the heart. Call it what you will: harmony, serenity, wholeness, soundness of mind — the yearning for it exists somewhere in every human being. No one likes problems, headaches, heartaches. Everyone wants peace—freedom from anxiety and doubt, violence and division. Everyone wants stability and security" [3]

Let us open our hearts to God and receive there—in the depths of our being —the peace God offers. This is the peace that comes to us when, through a spiritual birth, God liberates us from the dire consequences of self-preoccupation. It is, therefore, a peace that results from the cessation of the anxiety that drives us into friction with others.

With that very personal peacemaking task in process we are ready to move forward with God into a fractured and warring world to advance the cause of divine peace. For while peace begins within as peace in the soul with God, it moves outward to include, the fulfillment of nonviolence through peaceful relationships with others and the establishment of a just and peaceful social order.

As I contemplate the first phase of the outward movement of peacemaking —the fulfillment of nonviolence through peaceful relationships—I think of two particular stories, the first growing out of an experience with two pastoral colleagues and the other out of my own experience.

My colleagues were in Washington, D.C. for a professional conference. One evening they decided to visit a popular restaurant just off Capital Hill known not only for its excellent food but as a gathering place for political celebrities. Hailing a cab, they were soon speeding down the avenue when their cab approached a car going in the same direction in an adjacent lane. In that vehicle were two young adults—a white male and black female— who appeared to be highly agitated, arguing and gesturing wildly. Suddenly as their car came to a screeching halt the right side door flung open and was sheared off by the cab in which my colleagues were riding.

By the time their cab had stopped the two occupants of the other car were in the street yelling, screaming, and coming to blows. As one of my colleagues immediately left the cab and ran toward the scene another car with four young African American men stopped. My colleague yelled out to them, "Come on fellas, let's see if we can help these people!"

They all rushed to the scene and began reasoning with the couple who, in turn, stopped their fighting and settled into an awkward silence. The four young men and my colleague asked if they could be helpful to the couple who responded with a "We are going to be O.K. We're sorry for all the commotion but thankful that you cared enough to stop and give us help."

Later as my colleague processed the experience he said to his friend,

"I know my intervention was risky. I realized how risky when the young men in the other car stopped and started toward the scene. But my impulse was to establish rapport with them by inviting them to join me in determining if we could be helpful. It worked!

They immediately joined with me in what felt like an alliance with a goal toward reducing conflict between the couple. As I reflect upon it our intervention not only helped the couple, but it seemed to mold my alliance with perfect strangers in a way that reduced the socio-economic gap between us."

The other story I wish to share is one that grew out of my own personal experience at a fast-food restaurant in Ft. Lauderdale, Florida. My associate and I were traveling west on Oakland Park Boulevard when we spotted a McDonald's restaurant. Suddenly we shifted into the turn off lane in order to grab a bite to eat. We had entered the restaurant and were standing in line to place our order when a fellow raging with anger approached me and exclaimed, "You Motherf....., you cut me off out there in traffic!!"

My momentary stunned state gave me time to remember the wise counsel of one who had taught me not to meet hostility with hostility when you want civility. I had time also to remember that my goal is to be a peace maker. That settled me to respond, "Sir, I remember making a sudden decision to turn. Looking in my mirror and not seeing anyone, I changed lanes to turn into the restaurant. In the process it appears I cut you off and for that I am very sorry. It was not intentional, I assure you." He seemed to relax as I continued, "My relationship with you is so much more important to me than to try to justify my action. Please forgive me."

By now he appeared totally relaxed and responded, "O.K. Then. I forgive you."

Receiving our order, my associate and I took our seats in the restaurant. I looked up to see that the fellow had received his "to go" order and was heading for the door. As he proceeded he looked back at me, smiled and waved. I knew that peace had replaced hostility and that both of us—brothers in the human family—were better persons as we proceeded through the day.

These incidents, one in our nation's capital and the other in Ft. Lauderdale, illustrate styles of peacemaking in our everyday lives that can contribute to the goal of utilizing vulnerability, kindness and gentleness to dispel the cloud of hostility and enable peace to grow among us.

Peace within moves outwardly toward a goal of establishing peace in our every-day/ordinary relationship with others. It extends its outward reach in our efforts to establish a just and peaceful social order.

This extension brings us face to face with a warring spirit that has ensconced itself in our social and political systems. Mahatma Gandhi and Martin Luther King, Jr. are prime examples of the power of non-violent confrontation to transform unjust systems which breed a warring spirit into peace that recognizes human kinship and dignity out of which harmony and equality grow.

With great success in his wake and just prior to his assassination, Dr. King had begun to turn his civil rights movement toward the issue of war; particularly the war in Vietnam. He believed that as different races could live together in peace so might nations. Unfortunately his life was taken before he could mobilize toward that goal.

Hostility is alive and well in several dimensions of our social order today. Politically this nation has become so internally polarized that, at times, our political machinery is not able to function. War or the spirit of war is alive and well among nations in the Middle East, parts of Africa, and among many of our world's great nations. In the latter part of the 20th century and in our own, we have seen the resurrection of division and hostility between two of the world's great religions—Christianity and Islam.

The time is ripe for aggressive peacemaking at every level. Often I ask myself how can I, as one human being, affect the course of a world so full of the warring spirit. This sends me in search of others with whom I can combine my effort to produce a stronger impact for peace. I find them everywhere. Every major religious movement has an identifiable group whose goal is to enable world peace. And, existing alongside the efforts of religious movements, are non-religious groups who work for peace as well. As an American at the ballot box I am constantly searching for candidates who possess a spirit of peaceful co-existence across political lines in our own government as well as peaceful co-existence among nations. I am not looking particularly for those who practice traditional pacifism but for persons capable of discretion who seek wisely to discern when there are authentic openings for peace capable of mobilizing effective means of taking advantage of those openings.

Peace is always near the top of my prayer list. I earnestly believe the ancient promise given by God to Solomon is also meant for us:

> *"If my people who are called by my name humble themselves, pray, seek my face, and turn from their wicked ways, then I will hear from heaven, and will forgive their sin and heal their land. Now my eyes will be open and my ears attentive to the prayer that is*

made..." (11 Chronicles 7:14—New Revised Standard Version).

With millions of other faithful persons who pray the Lord's Prayer, the words, "...*Thy kingdom come, Thy will be done on earth as it is in heaven...,*" compel me to believe that God's will for our earth is to experience the ultimate quality of existence realized in heaven. That prayer motivates me to join God in the work toward that goal and to trust God to bring it into reality.

It is the task of peacemaking to explore every peace option and to expend dynamic energy in an effort to bring the world to experience the blessed desire God has for all creation. As I join the effort in a world so fractured with the warring spirit, I am aware that on the journey toward the triumph of world peace, God has provided me with an inner peace that is full and abundant even in the midst of the world's violence.

In the Bruderhof, a community that affirms and works for peace, each member is asked to affirm a pro-active covenant. Though I find it odd that each point of the covenant is couched in military imagery, I realize that the point is to emphasize the aggressive character of peacekeeping. The components of the covenant include the following:

> We declare war against all irreverence
> toward the childlike spirit of Jesus.
>
> We declare war against all emotional or
> physically cruelty toward children.
>
> We declare war against the search for
> power over the souls of others.
>
> We declare war against all human
> greatness and all forms of vanity.
>
> We declare war against all false pride,
> including collective pride.
>
> We declare war against the spirit of
> unforgiveness, envy, and hatred.
>
> We declare war against all cruelty to
> anyone, even if he or she has sinned.
>
> We declare war against all curiosity
> about magic or satanic darkness. [4]

In my view working for peace in the world cannot be avoided if one is serious about joining the Prince of Peace in one of his most precious endeavors. I want very much to be a part of that adventure and, therefore, to be a part of the solution rather than the problem.

Compassion for *Practicing Conservation*

The two creation stories appearing in chapters 1 and 2 of *Genesis* provide a theological foundation for the Judeo-Christian faith. That foundation is built upon not only through remaining chapters of *Genesis* but throughout the continuing books of the Bible. The conclusion of these works is that God is the timeless Creator, that God loves all creation and God has primacy over that creation.

Early in *Genesis* it becomes clear that God maintains a close relationship with creation and calls human beings to maintain that relationship as well. The writers seem to recognize that in order to meet that challenge, it is important for us to understand the nature and value of the created order.

Let us now zoom in for a closer view of God's evaluation of the created order and our relationship to it. There we will discover issues that are fundamental to a Judeo-Christian perspective: The Goodness of the Created Order (Nature), Our Responsibility Regarding Nature, a Distorted Perception of Our Responsibility, and the Practice of Conservation.

1. The *Goodness* of the Created Order

The perception of the goodness of creation is clear in the *Genesis* account. In the first of two creation stories God enters into several "acts" of creation: light, sky, land, sea, plants, lights in the sky (stars, Sun and Moon), living creatures to dwell in the water, birds and the various other animals both large and small, and, finally, human beings. As each "act" is completed it is followed by God's expression of pleasure—"*…and it was good.*" or "*…and God was pleased with what he saw.*"

Thus we have come to believe that all reality has come into being by the hand of God and that it is inherently good and pleasing. This affirmation of the goodness of creation is a distinctive feature of Judeo-Christian faith. Much of our thinking in the so-called western world has been influenced by Greek dualism which views materiality or physicality as evil and only the "soul" of something as good. (I suspect that some readers on hearing this will be surprised that Judeo-Christian faith does not support such a view.)

For God to pronounce nature as good is for God to place value upon it— whether a tree, rabbit, fish, or human being. It is good; therefore it has value, precious value.

Thankfully, there seems to be a growing consensus in society at large that the natural system is extremely precious and deserves our highest sensitivity to its preservation.

2. Our *Responsibility* for The Natural Order (Creation)

With its value in mind, it is not surprising that in the second story, God charges human beings with caring for the natural order:

(addressing human beings)… *"Have many children, so that your descendants will live all over the earth and bring it under their control. I am putting you in charge of the fish, the birds, and all the wild animals. I have provided all kinds of grain and all kinds of fruit for you to eat; but for all the wild animals and for the birds I have provided grass and leafy plants for food…."* (Genesis 1:28-30—Today's English Version).

It's as though God takes humankind out for a view of the natural order, to see its various species as creatures to be valued; then says to us, "You have responsibility for taking care of it."

As I write, my mind rushes back to the farm on which my brother and I were raised. Our Dad helped us till the soil and plant the seed but once the plants broke through the ground and waved their friendly wands toward us, Dad would say, "All right boys, its time for you to take care of it." We did, and the growing crops were things of beauty which not only served some of our aesthetic needs but sustained us physically.

Clearly, God's charge for us to take care of the natural order forms the basis of the doctrine of stewardship in the Judeo-Christian faith. There is a variety of ways in which that doctrine of taking care of things gets applied, ranging from soil conservation to financial offerings that support God's work here at home and abroad.

What God has always known, we are rapidly learning, namely, that creation is a beautiful arrangement and that in caring for it (practicing stewardship) we not only conserve it but we also find a well-spring of happiness, meaning and hope.

Unfortunately, this part of the story that describes our relationship to the natural order has been distorted by some who have interpreted it to be a reason to exploit and manipulate nature in destructive ways.

The rationale behind the distortion runs something like this: Humans are above nature— superior to it—therefore we have the right to do with it whatever we want. As a result we have ugly results—expanding deforestation that contributes both to the destruction of land and air, sprawling strip mining that leaves deep scars on the face of the land, the poaching of certain species of animals— elephants, rhinos, lions—which endangers their viability, water pollution and depletion, etc.

I remember a fellow who lived in a rural area near Newland, North Carolina. His house and land were in a prominent location that all could see as they made their way up the mountain on their way to the county seat.

One would think that with such prominence a land owner would take pride in presenting a pleasing view to passersby, but such was not the case with the old fellow who continued to trash the exterior walls of his house with an array of things ranging from automobile hubcaps to rusty chains and animal skins. His yard was covered with all kinds of junk from discarded refrigerators to rusting hulks of old cars. The areas of his yard not covered with the junk had become ugly weed patches.

There it was, this unsightly mess, that lay in stark contrast to the beautiful valley it overlooked. It was a "sight for sore eyes" many remarked and it "smelled to high heaven" others would add. So disgusted were many of the people in the county that they gave the owner the ironic name, "Sanitary Brown."

One day some concerned citizens went to "Sanitary" to request that he clean up his place and make it more presentable. They were met with stern resistance and a strong exclamation: "This is my place and I will do with it whatever I damn well please!!"

Sanitary Brown's comment represents the spirit of those who continue to ignore our responsibility to care for nature. The distortion's religious language is very similar to that of Sanitary— "If God didn't intend to us to exploit nature then why did he command us to "…*subdue it, and have dominion over it…?*"

Not everyone who abuses the natural order is driven by a distorted religious concept, particularly in our 21st century. It appears that there are great numbers of people who simply relate to nature carelessly. For example on the road to my community I frequently see the leftover fragments of food and containers which have been dumped onto the road. Such folk may not be intentionally abusive but their carelessness defies a sense of responsibility.

3. The *Practice* of Conservation

In spite of those who continue to abuse the natural order, whether intentionally or carelessly, I am delighted with the increasing numbers who are committed to conserving it.

I am particularly encouraged by the growing sense that we human beings are not superior to nature but a part of it; the thought that there is a strong kinship between humans and other parts of the animal kingdom and even between humans and the plant kingdom.

In his book, *The Future of Creation,* Theologian Jurgen Moltmann writes about the need for experiencing *inter*dependence within the created order and for affirming the symbiotic relationship between humans and the rest of nature:

> "Justice is the form of authentic interdependence between people and the environment. It comes into being in the symbioses between different systems of life, and is the basis for common survival. Its presupposition is the recognition and subjectivity of the other life systems....We human persons need each other within communities—need each other with the community of mankind. We—the creation— need God, our Creator and Redeemer.

Mankind faces the urgent task of devising social mechanisms and political structures that encourage genuine interdependence, in order to replace mechanisms and structures that sustain domination and subservience"[5]

In his book, *The Nature Principle,* Richard Louv raises the issue of our (human) relationship with other species in nature. He acknowledges that human beings are part of nature and capable of relating to other species both in giving and receiving. His vision is of a relationality between ourselves and other forms of nature that paints a different picture than any derived from the assumption that humans are superior to and masters of other species of creation.

For example, Louv believes that the development of what he calls "an ecological unconscious" is feeding this inter-relational dynamic:

"The idea of an 'ecological unconscious' now hovers above the crossroads of science, philosophy, and theology—the notion that all of nature is connected in ways we do not fully understand. In his 1841 essay, 'The Over Soul,' Ralph Waldo Emerson wrote of 'that great nature in which we rest, as themselves earth lies in the soft arms of the atmosphere, that

> every man's particular being is constrained and made
> one with all other, the common heart'"[6]

Both Moltmann's and Louv's remarks describe an interdependency and commonality among nature's species that resist the adversarial imagery of power invasions from vantage points of superiority that attempt to control, exploit and abuse nature. In doing so, they help us better to understand the character of the relationship between ourselves and the rest of nature.

I believe that in every nation and in the leadership of those nations, we humans are experiencing a growing concern for the natural order reflected in our strategies for conservation. This concern gained enormous impetus from those pictures received from early space travelers of earth bathed in blue against the darkness of surrounding space. As a result and in unprecedented ways we have begun to think of the earth as a ship on which billions are traveling and, therefore, as a dwelling place whose resources need to be wisely managed and sensibly conserved.

In our own nation (USA) we have an entity called the *Environmental Protection Agency* whose existence and focus remind us all that to take care of our planet and beyond is an imperative we cannot ignore.

As I've grown through the years I am much more sensitive to the need to conserve our water supply and the quality of the air. When I see water being wasted or air being polluted, I feel a sense of urgency to do something about it.

When I look at the magnificent forests from the vantage point of an airplane, I am thankful for the wisdom of local, state, and federal efforts to preserve them, not only for their oxygen production and protectors of topsoil, but also for their role in satisfying the needs of animals and plants and, as parks and wilderness, their role in keeping us humans in touch with nature.

My sensitivity to animals and plants sometimes surprises me. My wonderful nine year old "Yorkie" has helped me hone my kinship with animals. The landscaping that surrounds where we live, including the preserve that unfolds behind our house, are teaching me not only to respect the plant kingdom, but to interrelate with it.

As I perform such service I experience the exhilaration of being set free from the selfpreoccupation that breeds the leech-like sucking of my spirit's blood and the sensation that comes from remarkable fulfillment. I have a growing conviction that an important part of the work for which I have been set free is to value, affirm, and conserve the remarkable natural order of which God has made us a part and with which we are surrounded.

Compassion for *Sharing the Story*

Let's imagine for a moment that we are looking from a hilltop at a great expanse of land. On the East we see the base of the mountains sloping into it, bordered on the West by a large body of water. At first we are struck by the scene's majesty; then we notice some very unusual activity all across the earthen floor. Closer examination reveals thousands of whirlpools of different sizes whirling with such intensity that everything surrounding them—ponds of water, grass, bushes animals and the like—are being sucked into their vortex. Some of the whirlpools are even consuming other whirlpools. All across the expanse can be heard a giant sucking sound as more and more stuff disappears. We fear that the land is consuming itself, and we grow very anxious.

I use this imaginative picture as a parable to describe what is occurring within and among us emotionally and spiritually. Somewhere in our history —perhaps from the beginning—we became anxious about our own security. As the anxiety became more powerful it drove (and drives) us to exploit our surroundings in order to feed our insecurity's raging appetite. The energy of that project turns us into virtual whirlpools attempting to pull everything and everyone into ourselves in order to secure our own existence. Any recognition of God's care or the sacred dignity of other humans or other species within the natural order is dulled—if not obliterated—by our intense commitment to exploiting everything and everyone for ourselves.

This project to secure ourselves is fed by our growing anxiety and guilt. Eventually we feel trapped and begin to realize that we are victims and that the selfish project has become our prison.

The images of this whirlpool parable come very close to describing the dynamics and consequences of what our faith tradition calls sin. Consider, for example the story of Adam and Eve, symbols of our human race. In the Garden of Eden, God provides them with an amazing security but that secure situation does not make them invulnerable to temptation. They are pictured as wanting more than they think they have. The temptation to which they eventually succumb appeals precisely to their desire to be equal with God and, therefore, more secure in their existence (read the story for yourself in Genesis 3:1-13).

From the story we can discern that the ongoing project to secure our own existence involves the elevation of the self above all other considerations and moves us to perceive others as adversaries to be outdone and overcome.

The Biblical story proceeds from this ancient commentary on the existential dilemma in which we humans are caught to an exploration of God's design to fix us at our core. The sixty six books of the Bible are very descriptive of God's efforts. The Old Testament provides a narrative of God's plan whose salient points contain the choosing of Abraham who will produce a people (Israel) through whom God will bless the world, the provision of a Law (particularly the ten commandments) to guide human behavior, and the provision of prophets to make known God's will for the people, These prophets project into the future God's plan for a Messiah through whom God will ultimately eradicate all the distortion which sin injected into human existence. Messiah's work will result in the restoration of the harmony for which all of creation was designed.

The New Testament picks up from the prophets this messianic hope. Its four Gospels focus upon the coming of the Messiah, identifying him as Jesus. They proceed to describe his ministry, death, and resurrection. *The Acts of the Apostles* and the Letters of St. Paul and others describe the birth of the Church, its development in the first century, along with elaborations on the significance of Christ's work for the world's destiny. The book of *Revelation* provides an interesting interpretation of the clash between the forces of evil and the Spirit of God along with a splendid description of God's victory.

The writer of *The Letter to the Hebrews* gives us a succinct summary of God's plan in these words:

> *"In the past God spoke to our ancestors many times and in many ways through the prophets, but in these last days he has spoken to us through his Son. He is the one*

through whom God created the universe, the one whom God has chosen to possess all things at the end. He reflects the brightness of God's glory and is the exact likeness of God's own being, sustaining the universe with his powerful word. After achieving forgiveness for the sins of all human beings, he sat down in heaven at the right side of God, the supreme Power" (Hebrews 1:1-3— Today's English Version).

Together these stories of God's rescuing response to our human predicament constitute what our faith calls the *Gospel* (meaning "Good News"), which has become a bright shining star in the dark sky of bad news about our condition.

In short, the story of our faith involves a recognition that we human beings are wandering in a wilderness of lostness. But the story also includes God's solution announced by faithful leaders of Israel leading to the unprecedented work of Jesus Christ whose coming gives us a clear picture of God's unconditional love and, at the same time, draws us to that love in such a way that we are recreated as new persons. It's as though, in our experience of Jesus, God peers over the portals of heaven and shouts to us: "You are loved, not condemned. I accept you warts and all, and I am determined to earn your trust which will liberate you from self-destruction and transform you into wholeness!"

Out of his experience of that unlimited ocean of grace which resides in the bosom of God, Jesus put it this way: *"For God so loved the world that he gave his only Son, so that everyone who believes in him may not perish, but have eternal life. Indeed, God did not send the Son into the world to condemn the world, but in order that the world might be saved through him"* (John 3:16-17—New Revised Standard Version).

That's a description of the Gospel story that comes to us from the pages of Holy Scripture and in confirmed in the experience of millions who have heard the Good News of God and have responded positively to it.

Continuously, this story must be shared. Every generation has a responsibility to tell it. The African-American spiritual encourages the community of believers in these words,

> "Go tell it on the mountain, over the
> hills and everywhere; Go tell it on the
> mountain, that Jesus Christ is born!"

In his *Letter to the Romans,* sharing his conviction that God's salvation for the world provided in Jesus Christ is for everyone, St Paul declares:

> *"'…Everyone who calls of the name of the Lord shall be saved.' But how are they to call on one in whom they have not believed? And how are they to hear without someone to proclaim him? And how are they to*

proclaim him unless they are sent? As it is written, 'How beautiful are the feet of those who bring good news!' (10:13-15—New Revised Standard Version).

The great apostle's firm belief is that God wants to rescue everyone; that, therefore, all who have been found and delivered are encouraged to share the story that everyone else will hear the Good News and be drawn to it. Moreover, he notes that those who who share the story are living a life of beauty!

Earlier Jesus declares to us: *"All authority in heaven and on earth has been given to me. Go therefore and make disciples of all nations…"* (Matthew 28:l8-19a—New Revised Standard Version). In this preamble to what we know as the Great Commission, Jesus is directing believers in all places and times to share the Good News of God that people everywhere will be rescued from going down the drain of their self-made whirlpools.

There are other compelling reasons for us to recommit ourselves to sharing the Gospel story. These seem especially relevant:

Telling the Story Is Every

Generation's Responsibility.

Our Fractured World Is in Need of Healing.

Modern Technology Provides Us

with Unprecedented Opportunities
for Communicating the Story.
We Are Surrounded by Spiritual Hunger.

These are of such crucial importance I want to focus a little more closely on each one:

1. Telling the Story Is Every Generation's Responsibility

Like all stories the Good News of the Gospel must be communicated constantly. If one generation drops the ball that goal could be missed. Thankfully since it came into being over several centuries, reaching its climax in Jesus as the Christ, the Gospel story has been told and retold with such clarity that in these early years of the 21st century it's effect continues to be dynamically life-giving.

Because the story has proven to be the most powerful influence in our world, affecting the direction and quality of life for millions, we seem determined to pass it on to neighbors both far and near.

As a father, I told the story to my children. Now, as a grandfather, I utilize every opportunity to share it with my grandchildren. I see this happening with friends and acquaintances as well, and that excites me.

It is important for future generations to shoulder the responsibility of sharing the story with their children and grandchildren, neighbors and friends. Such possibility makes me hopeful that as long as time goes on, the story will remain alive and its life-giving blessing will be showered upon people everywhere.

2.   Our Fractured World Is in *Need of Healing*

We are all aware that our world is severely wounded and broken. Every community, city, and continent reflects this dilemma. Poverty continues to be rampant in this relatively affluent period. Addictions are as prevalent as raindrops in a storm. Estrangement invades marriage and family life, tearing those who have experienced the beauty of love and intimacy from one another's arms and hearts. Nations are suspicious of one another and spend inordinate amounts of time and other resources in an effort to seek advantage. Ebola and other ravaging diseases are seeking more and more people to devour. Terrorism has spawned a poisonous cloud that hangs over every nation. In short, our world is in trouble, a victim of violence and injustice. It lies wounded and bleeding in the ditch beside the road just as surely as that person who in one of Jesus' stories was ignored by potential helpers until the Good Samaritan came along and cared enough to respond with compassion.

We must not forget to share the story. Our society needs to hear the message and its words. If the story is ever forgotten, the world may become hopeless. Let us live in constant awareness that sharing the story of God's rescue presented in the Good News of the Gospel is to make available a divine and human compassion that can bring healing and wholeness.

3.   Modern Technology Provides *Unprecedented Opportunities* for Sharing the Story

Some years ago as I stood on the spot of Jesus' Sermon on the Mount I thought of the logistics of communicating with such a vast crowd without the aid of microphones and amplifiers. Could people located farthest from him hear what he was saying? What about those who were hard of hearing? How loudly did Jesus have to speak? Did he strain his voice?

I thought, too, of how his disciples shared what they had learned from Jesus. There was no efficient postal system that could deliver letters soon after they were written; no telephones, no e-mail capability.

But Jesus was heard and what he had to say got communicated effectively to his generation and beyond. Not only did all in the small land of Israel hear of him, but all of what we now call the Middle East and Europe. In fact all the "known world" heard the message including, according to legends surrounding Thomas, India, and all this within the first century!

Now shift forward into our own time and just think of how the Good News of the Gospel is being communicated across the entire globe and into space on the wings of our amazing technological capability.

Through social media one person can reach more people in a moment than could be reached in the entire first century. People of faith everywhere are sharing experiences about the liberating love of God. Long range counseling sessions are constantly occurring as people with all kinds of physical and mental maladies are being nurtured back to health.

People of faith are becoming increasingly savvy about the use of technology in sharing the story with others who are both far and near. Never before have so many had the opportunity to hear about God's love. Thankfully there are many believers who, out of their deep compassion, are utilizing every means to tell that story.

Though there is considerable bad news in our world, the Good News of God's story is being increasingly amplified. The expression of that Good News is stretching beyond traditional means such as sermons and is now finding expression in so-called secular literature and drama. Some of the most popular television programs and movies these days are carriers of the Good News of God's love.

I am convinced that God is at work in our world. As increasing millions become co-workers with God,

I experience a growing trust that Jesus' prayer: "… *Thy kingdom come, Thy will be done, on earth as it is in heaven….*" is in process of being answered.

4. There Is Widespread *Spiritual Hunger*

Every poll I see confirms that there is a deep yearning for meaning and purpose, both of which, lie at the center of the spiritual quest. These polls, at the same time, clarify that many of these persons are not turning toward traditional forms organized or institutional religion. In fact, they indicate a declining interest in such forms.

The situation has important implications for those of us who are committed to sharing the Good News story. On the one hand, it tells us that millions are searching for something deeper than what materialism, consumerism, and secularism have to offer. Their quest is for that which can give meaning to their lives and fill them with a sense of purpose. At the same time, the situation tells us that we must be creative in our approach to sharing the story and not get stuck in ways and means that have grown irrelevant or otherwise have become blocking forces to that sharing.

As a believer I am convinced that such quest can be met in an encounter with God and participation in a community of faith. I experience a growing conviction that Jesus' counsel to *"…seek first the Kingdom of God and all these other things will be added unto you"* is right on the mark. I am also convinced that God's plan includes the fulfilling potential of joining with others in community or fellowship. That communal experience rescues us from isolation and plants us with fellow human beings among whom love, acceptance, trust, and purpose are explored and practiced. Together, this rescue and planting become genuine guides to finding our meaning and purpose.

Far from being a time of spiritual withering, ours is a time of deep spiritual vibrancy. I sense that believers everywhere are hearing with fresh ears the exciting vision of Jesus expressed in his declaration, *"…I tell you, look around you, and see how the fields are ripe for harvesting"* (John 4:35b— New Revised Standard Version).

CONCLUSION

It is not difficult to make the case that destructive anxiety is pervasive among us. Most every reader gets that! I have found the more difficult task is persuading readers that faith can be one of our most potent weapons in our arsenal for defeating anxiety.

British historian A.J. Toynbee, sensing this difficulty, wrote: "How, then, can we arrive at a true, and therefore lasting peace?. ...For true and lasting peace, a religious revolution is, I am sure, a sine qua non. By religion I mean the overcoming of self-centeredness, in both individuals and communities, by getting into communion with the spiritual presence behind the universe and by bringing our wills into harmony with it. I think this is the only key to peace, but we are very far from picking up this key and using it, and, until we do, the survival of the human race will continue to be in doubt."[1]

Because I believe there continues to be great spiritual hunger in the land, along with a growing realization that the complexity of our problems, demands something "beyond" our own strength for solution, this book represents my hopeful and enthusiastic attempt to make the case for a faithful alliance with God and God's desire for the world as an effective remedy for our dilemma.

I recognize that moving into such alliance is not simple or easy. A deep sense of insecurity and its resulting anxiety, much like a straight jacket, bind us with such mistrust that movement toward the alternative becomes a strong challenge. Such movement may seem improbable from a purely rational point of view. However, when genuine faith is introduced into the equation, we are positioned to behold the "miracle" of trusting God's care, along with its power to penetrate the fetters of our bondage, weakening them in such a way that we are able to break free and proceed toward God.

God's awesome grace, therefore, gives birth to our trust. It is not as though, under our own power, we convince ourselves that God can help; then proceed to break the bonds and move toward God. It is God who plants the seed of hope, weakens our binding fetters, and sets us free for an adventure of radical trust which becomes a continuous and growing process within us.

Two prayers, one by 12th century's St. Francis of Assisi and another by 20th century's Reinhold Niebuhr reflect the positive state of mind and being which follows in the wake of our surrender to and alliance with God:

A Simple Prayer

Lord, make me an instrument of your peace.
Where there is hatred…let me sow love
Where there is injury…pardon,
Where there is doubt…faith,
Where there is darkness…light,
Where there is sadness…joy.

O Divine Master, grant that I may not so much seek
To be consoled……as to console,
To be understood…as to understand,
To be loved……as to love, for
It is in giving……that we receive,
It is in pardoning…that we are pardoned, It is
in dying…that we are born to eternal life.

St. Francis

The Serenity Prayer

God grant me the serenity to accept the things
I cannot change; courage to change the things I
can; and wisdom to know the difference. Living
one day at a time; Enjoying one moment at a time;
Accepting hardships as the pathway to peace;
Taking as He did, the sinful world
as it is, not as I would have it;
Trusting that He will make all wrong
right if I surrender to His will;
So that I may be reasonably happy in
this life and supremely happy with
Him forever in the next. Amen

We who have traded a life of anxiety to live in the dimension of God's care find ourselves resonating with the spirit and thought of these prayers while identifying and articulating our own description of what that looks and feels like.

For me, the foundation of that blessed state of being is God's unconditional love that has the power to transform our shivering preoccupation into integrity, balance, and compassion. In other words, experience tells me that, in spite of my imperfection, God has come to live within me, closer than my own breathing, and that the work to which God calls me is life-giving both to me and the world around me.

This blessed state of being does not insulate me from the crises of life. I feel pain when life strikes me a blow or when pain and misfortune come to others. However, when the pain comes, I am provided both meaning and endurance, along with trusting wisdom to direct me through any temporary maze in which I may be caught.

I offer the following story to illustrate the secure state of being into which God invites us:

Through my childhood village flowed a beautiful stream called Elk River. Normally its clear waters meandered though the valley bordered on either side by tall mountains. In some places, where its waters cascaded over and through rocky terrain, they swirled noisily only to settle down in pools of refreshing quietness. But during an extremely rainy season the Elk could swell into a raging brown torrent capable of pushing huge boulders around like chips of wood, gnawing at the shoreline, and grabbing entire houses to float them into oblivion. Flood times were very concerning to all of the village inhabitants.

During such events I found solace in my Dad's loving care. I sensed that Dad's purpose was not to prevent the flood. His role was spelled out by the presence of those loving arms into which he gathered my brother and me. Moreover, his reassurance that the flood had higher purposes than its obvious destruction, his special provision of adequate supplies, and his wise reflections on whether to move to higher ground were enough for me to feel secure.

Repeatedly I have found such reassurance in God. I don't expect God to insulate me from the hurts of life. What I find extremely settling, however, is the experience of God delivering me through those hurts to find meaning both in the experience of the pain and the exhilaration of the deliverance.

It is that experience I hope for readers of this work. Trusting God's care is the means by which we are liberated from bondage and set upon an adventure of abundant living.

I'm aware that there are those of us who suspect that if we allow ourselves to become intentionally faithful we may have to settle for living in the narrow end of a funnel cone, restricted physically, intellectually, and spiritually from experiencing the full potential of what it means to be human.

To those who have such apprehension I want to reaffirm my experience that to trust God is not confining. I find that intentional faith has been the medium for my own expansion toward the spirit of inquiry, learning, and openness. For me, reliance upon God's care and being intentional about spiritual disciplines have moved me to live beyond the cone, farther and farther away from its narrowness.

I have a clear hope for you. If you haven't already, may you experience an intentional trust in God and God's care, trust capable of rescuing you from constant anxiety-ridden turmoil and introducing you to a the "still waters," the "green pastures," and walking without fear through the "valley of shadows" of which Psalm 23 speaks so eloquently. Those who experience such transformation discover life to be a splendid journey filled with security, purpose, direction, compassion, growth and hope; all within this tumultuous world which needs the strength of such stability.

There is this beautiful promise In Isaiah 40 that captures the blessing of gathering our individual and corporate lives under the umbrella of God's grace:

> *"Don't you know? Haven't you heard? The Lord is the everlasting God; he created all the world. He never grows tired or weary. No one understands his thoughts. He strengthens those who are weak and tired. Even those who are young grow weak; young people can fall exhausted.*
>
> *But those who trust in the Lord for help will find their strength renewed. They will rise up on wings like eagles; they will run and not get weary; they will walk and not grow weak"* (Isaiah 40:28-31—Today's English Version).

Go now and fly with eagle's wings!

END

NOTES

Chapter One

[1] As used here, the word "faith" refers not to a belief system but, in the biblical sense, a radical trust in God's trustworthiness and care. This distinction is made clear in John Caputo's article "A Restless Search for Truth" in the December 24, 2014 issue of *The Christian Century.* There he writes, "I make a distinction between faith and belief. Belief is a proposition, a creed formed by a council, leaders agreeing on a belief system. I don't think creeds are unimportant, but I think they rigidify. To be true to faith, you have to keep those things flexible and recognize their contingency. What matters is the form

of life, what Heidegger called our mode of being in the world. Belief systems can't capture this. They tend to congeal, contract, and rigidify faith. Faith is a deeper and more fundamental structure (pp. 31,32).

Chapter Two

[1] From my perspective, particular *belief systems* have evolved from experiences of relying on God and are, therefore, intellectual distillations of our deeper *faith*. Dogma and doctrines become important symbols we utilize to reference faith's meaning, but they are mere (and helpful) symbols.

That to which we are called by God, the level of experience that frees us from our insecurity and its attending anxiety lies deep below our traditional systems, those points at which our human spirit enters into relationship with God.

To enhance the richness of our spiritual being it is important for us to distinguish between the symbols and the experience of relating to God. Such a distinction helps us to draw from the content of the symbols while setting us free from fixation with them to explore the depth of our relationship with God.

In this context I find considerable significance in a cautionary statement by Joyce Carol Oates: *"Homo Sapiens* is the species that invents symbols in which to invest power and authority and then forgets that symbols are inventions."

("The Calendar's New Clothes," *New York Times,* December 30, 1999).

Chapter Three

1 Victor E. Frankl, *Man's Search for Ultimate Meaning,* (New York: Basic Books, 2000) pp. 84,85

2 Jonathan Christopher Arnold, *Seeking Peace,* (Farmington, Pennsylvania: Plough Publishing House, 1998) p. xv

3 Ibid, p. xv

4 Ibid, pp. 30,31

5 Jurgen Moltmann, *The Future of Creation*: Fortress Press, Philadelphia, 1979) p. 79

6 Robert Louv, *The Nature Principle*, Algonguin Books, Chapel Hill 2012) p. 62

7 A.J. Toynbee, Surviving the Future, London/New York/Toronto, 1971, pp. 44-45